I0530055

AI for Personal Development

Harnessing Artificial Intelligence to Accelerate Growth, Resilience, and Emotional Mastery

John Workman, Ph.D.

Book 1 of The AI Enhance Living Series

Please consult a licensed professional before attempting any techniques outlined in this book.

By reading this document, the reader agrees that under no circumstances is the author responsible for any direct or indirect losses incurred as a result of the use of the information contained within this document, including, but not limited to, errors, omissions, or inaccuracies.

Foreword

There was a moment not long ago when I found myself reflecting deeply on a conversation between two colleagues. One expressed concern about the growing presence of artificial intelligence in our everyday lives, while the other spoke with excitement about the limitless possibilities it could offer. I sat quietly, absorbing both perspectives, until it struck me: we were asking the wrong question. It wasn't about whether AI would change our lives; it already had. The real question was how we could shape that change to enhance our human experience, not diminish it.

That was the moment the idea for this book took root.

In a world increasingly driven by algorithms and data, artificial intelligence is no longer confined to the realm of science fiction or specialized industries. From virtual assistants guiding our schedules to recommendation systems curating our learning, AI now inhabits the spaces where we think, decide, and grow. But somewhere in the narrative about automation and efficiency, our personal inner growth, goals, and self-understanding have often been overlooked.

This book was born from the conviction that artificial intelligence, far from being a detached technological force, can serve as a partner in personal evolution. Whether it's helping us recognize cognitive patterns, track our habits, or simulate decision-making scenarios, AI holds the potential to sharpen our self-awareness and strengthen our capacity for lifelong growth. My intention in writing this work was to demystify that process, making it accessible to individuals who are not only curious about AI but also committed to becoming better versions of themselves.

I invite you to explore the chapters ahead not as passive reading, but as a journey, a practical framework for aligning technological tools with deeply human goals. In doing so, you will find that AI is not just reshaping the world around us; it can also help us reshape ourselves from within.

Let this be the beginning of that transformation.

John Workman, Ph.D.

Dedication

T o Dr. Diane Moore-Eubanks, Esq.

Some people influence our lives through grand gestures. You did it with a single sentence, spoken in passing yet filled with clarity and conviction:
"You're too smart just to be a realtor."

What you likely intended as a moment of encouragement became a profound turning point for me. Those words echoed in my thoughts long after our conversation ended, planting the seed for a new path, one that led to a deeper exploration of human potential, and ultimately, this very book.

Your insight pierced through the ordinary and made me see myself through a new lens. You saw the scholar before I fully recognized him. You recognized the thinker behind the practitioner. And most importantly, you named what I had not yet dared to name for myself.

This book is more than a contribution to the conversation on artificial intelligence and personal development. It is a symbol of transformation, one that began with the gift of your words, your friendship, and your belief in what was possible.
With deepest gratitude and enduring respect, I dedicate this work to you.

Epigraph

A rtificial intelligence is not here to replace the human spirit; it is here to help us meet it more fully, with clarity, courage, and consciousness. It is not the end of human thought, but the beginning of a new kind of self-discovery, a mirror that reflects not only what we do, but who we can become."

John Workman, Ph.D.

Introduction

AI for Personal Development

W e are living in a moment of remarkable technological transformation. Artificial intelligence, once a topic confined to laboratories and science fiction, now inhabits the contours of our daily routines from the apps that manage our calendars to the algorithms that shape our news feeds. But as AI becomes increasingly embedded in how we work, learn, and interact, a question of deeper importance arises: Can this technology be harnessed not just to optimize what we do, but to elevate who we are?

This book explores that question with urgency and optimism. It is rooted in the belief that artificial intelligence, when thoughtfully applied, can become a powerful ally in our personal development. It is not a replacement for human intuition, growth, or willpower but a complement to them. It is a tool that, if used deliberately, can help us build self-awareness, enhance cognitive habits, and pursue our goals with greater clarity andefficiency.

The idea for this work began as a simple reflection on how AI already shapes our decisions in subtle, often unnoticed ways. I realized that if machines can learn from us, we should also learn to grow with them intentionally. Rather than fear a future dominated by artificial systems, we can engage with AI as a reflective surface, revealing patterns, preferences, and possibilities we might otherwise overlook.

In the chapters ahead, we'll explore a wide range of applications:
• How natural language models can help us journal, reflect, and reshape inner narratives.
• How data-driven platforms can support habit formation, goal tracking, and cognitive training.
• How tools once reserved for corporations like machine learning and predictive analytics can be adapted for individual insight and empowerment.
• And how ethical and mindful integration of AI can help preserve what is most human in us.

This is not a manual on coding or engineering. Nor is it a naive celebration of technology. It is a practical and philosophical guide for those who wish to grow with purpose in an age of machines. Whether you are an educator, entrepreneur, student, or simply someone curious about how to live more consciously in a digital world, this book is for you.

My goal is not to tell you what AI will do next. I invite you to consider what you can do differently, more wisely, by working with it.

How tools once reserved for corporations, like machine learning and predictive analytics, can be adapted for individual insight and empowerment.

Let's begin.

Ch. 1 - Understanding AI: Foundations for Human-Machine Collaboration

T he concept of a world where machines assist in problem-solving while understanding human language and identifying data patterns feels remarkable. Artificial Intelligence, or AI, powers the operation of this world. Understanding AI, both through its capabilities and limitations, is crucial before examining its potential to help with personal development.

The fundamental principle of AI is to build machines that replicate human thought processes and intelligence. These systems have programming that enables them to think and learn like the human brain, yet lack both consciousness and genuine understanding. AI functions through its use of algorithms and predefined rules while processing input data. AI functions like a talented apprentice that acquires knowledge from examples instead of having built-in intelligence and emotions.

People often underestimate how long AI development extends in history. In the 1950s, computer scientist Alan Turing raised a fundamental question in his seminal paper "Computing Machinery and Intelligence" when he asked, "Can machines think?" Through this investigation, Alan Turing established the Turing Test, which evaluates whether machines can demonstrate intelligent behavior that humans cannot differentiate from human actions. (The Turing Test, proposed by Alan Turing in 1950, is a method for evaluating a machine's ability to exhibit intelligent behavior indistinguishable from that of a human (AI Milestones: A Comprehensive Look at Artificial Intelligence Evolution). If a human evaluator cannot reliably tell the machine apart from another human based solely on conversation, the machine is said to have passed the test. (Turing test – Generative AI Commons. https://genaicommons.org/glossary/turing-test/)

The term "Artificial Intelligence" was introduced by John McCarthy who is known as the "father of AI" then he organized the significant 1956 Dartmouth Conference that marked the beginning of modern AI research. From their perspective these pioneers held that a precise description of human reasoning would allow its mechanization which sparked a decades-long research effort still ongoing today.

Let's look at some everyday examples. Interacting with Spotify's playlist recommendations or Facebook's targeted advertisements lets you experience narrow AI (Narrow AI refers to systems designed to perform specific tasks, such as recommending music or analyzing customer inquiries with high efficiency but limited flexibility (Exploring the Transformative Power of Artificial Intelligence). In contrast, General AI envisions a machine capable of replicating the full range of human cognitive abilities across any domain (Can Artificial Intelligence Replace Human Intelligence Ppt?). While narrow AI is widely used today, general AI remains a theoretical ambition that has not yet been realized.)

It excels at tasks including musical preference recognition and ad appeal prediction. Customer service chatbots and virtual assistants such as Siri and Alexa represent types of AI technology. Such systems analyze natural language inputs and demonstrate partial contextual understanding while delivering intuitive responses.

Many people incorrectly believe AI systems have autonomous thinking and consciousness abilities. That's not the case. AI systems do not experience emotions and do not form desires or make ethical evaluations. AI lacks human understanding but operates by recognizing patterns to generate data-based predictions. An AI system estimating your future purchase does not comprehend your emotional connection to items but detects patterns from your historical buying actions.

Understanding the various branches of AI proves beneficial for grasping their distinct purposes and functions. Machine Learning (ML), as a transformative subset of AI technology, allows systems to gain knowledge from data without requiring explicit instructions. Deep Learning (DL) enhances neural network models through multiple layers that mimic human brain architecture to detect intricate patterns. (Deep Learning is a subset of machine learning that structures algorithms in multiple layers, resembling a network of interconnected neurons (2019). Singapore : NUS deep-learning AI system puts Singapore on the global map of big data analytics. MENA Report). This layered design allows the system to recognize intricate patterns in data, such as identifying faces in photographs or understanding spokenlanguage.)

Think of how image recognition algorithms can identify a cat or a face in a photo. Meanwhile, Symbolic AI, the older approach, involves hand-coding sets of rules for machines to follow. Each paradigm has strengths: ML and DL excel at adapting to new information, while Symbolic AI shines when clear rules govern the domain
The term "Artificial Intelligence" represents a wide range of

concepts that can lead to confusion. People often picture robots and futuristic machines that function through autonomous decision-making. Popular images of AI generate excitement but today's AI technologies mostly function as straightforward recommendation systems and voice assistants which focus on specific tasks. "Narrow AI" refers to AI systems engineered to complete specific tasks. The advanced concept of "general AI" which aims to replicate all human intellectual abilities remains theoretical and has not been developed yet.

Platforms like Hugging Face exemplify how natural language processing models facilitate human-computer interaction. These tools can help draft emails, summarize articles, or answer questions, yet they do not possess understanding or consciousness. They analyze language patterns and generate responses based on vast amounts of data, but they do not "comprehend" in the human sense.

The identification of artificial intelligence limitations led to the development of a crucial field known as explainable AI (XAI). Complex AI systems require a detailed understanding of their decision-making processes when they impact essential areas such as healthcare, employment, and criminal justice systems. XAI works to make AI decision-making processes understandable while preserving human oversight and building trust in these advanced systems. The transparency of AI systems builds user confidence and ensures that technology meets ethical requirements for accountability.

Understanding these distinctions is essential. When you understand AI's potential and limitations, you can use it intentionally to achieve better results. AI does not pose a danger, nor does it take over your role, but it acts as an ally whose power you can unlock through proper comprehension to strengthen your capabilities. Your understanding of AI's true capabilities allows you to build a foundation for personal advancement through digital tools that support emotional mastery and resilience. (Emotional mastery describes the capacity to identify and comprehend one's feelings while controlling emotional responses successfully. Through the use of self-awareness tools that AI technologies facilitate, people can build resilience and maintain emotional balance while responding to life's challenges with improved clarity and intention.)

Understanding AI capabilities is vital when using AI systems to support personal growth. AI's capabilities are impressive yet often misunderstood. The primary strength of AI lies in its ability to process large data sets while finding patterns and predicting outcomes. The powerful AI capabilities enable self-improvement by delivering personalized feedback and insights that help accelerate emotional mastery and build resilience.
Visualize having a personal coach who monitors your daily routines and mood changes while tracking your progress in real-time. Through the analysis of extensive data, including journal entries and fitness statistics, AI reveals hidden patterns in social interactions that humans cannot detect. AI technology offers routine modification advice while providing tailored mindfulness exercises for stress management and supports long-term emotional response tracking. Data-driven insights turn personal development into a strategic process by eliminating guesswork.

The transformation depends heavily on machine learning capabilities. The system learns from fresh data continuously while refining its guidance over time. AI-powered meditation apps begin with basic mindfulness routines but evolve to match your specific stress triggers and preferences as they gather more data about you.

(Mindfulness exercises aim to maintain focus on current experiences through methods that include breathing practices, body scanning exercises, and meditation routines. Personal development programs that use AI find these exercises valuable because they develop awareness and emotional regulation while decreasing stress.) With ongoing use, it generates more customized advice, which forms an active feedback loop that maintains your connection to changing aspirations and emotional requirements.

However, it's important to recognize AI's limitations. AI demonstrates remarkable capabilities but remains unable to duplicate human emotions or replicate intuitive and moral understanding. AI functions only through algorithms and data because it does not possess consciousness or real understanding. While AI systems have the ability to examine mood patterns and recommend coping techniques, they lack the capacity for genuine empathy towards your emotions and understanding of the detailed context surrounding your personal experiences. The tool demonstrates advanced capabilities, yet it cannot replace human empathy and understanding.

Recognizing AI capabilities and boundaries allows you to deploy it purposefully. You can view AI as a personal mirror because it shows you your habits, emotional patterns, and developmental progress. Applying AI correctly enables you to identify development opportunities and discover actionable strategies while providing accountability support. Human judgment, along with your empathy, creativity, and core values, should direct your interpretation and actions based on these insights. Understanding AI's capabilities and limitations enables you to establish practical expectations and develop trust in its potential. You can view AI as a personal development partner because it strengthens your skills while offering assistance to overcome challenges. The initial step to merging AI into your self-improvement journey requires ethical and strategic understanding while ensuring your personal development becomes intentional and resilient.

Envision starting your day knowing that an unseen, powerful helper is persistently working for you to improve your decision-making skills and track your progress while revealing personal insights you would not notice. That's the promise of artificial intelligence. Which specific functions does AI perform, and what are its genuine areas of proficiency?

AI's primary strength lies in its ability to quickly process massive amounts of data. AI can detect patterns in numerical data, textual information, visual content, and behavioral trends much faster than humans, who would need years to notice such patterns (Leveraging AI for Customer Behavior Prediction in Digital Marketing). AI analyzes thousands of your written records, including journal entries and social media posts, to track emotional patterns and reveal how your feelings change throughout your life. This technology analyzes extensive data collections to forecast your upcoming requirements while offering tailored guidance for achieving your objectives.

Machine learning stands as one of artificial intelligence's transformative elements. Machine learning functions like a digital apprentice that grows through experience. Tracking your meditation practice through an AI-powered app helps it identify your most relaxed times of day and best techniques while detecting when you're most likely to miss sessions. The AI system continually refines its recommendations based on your evolving habits to enhance personal growth efficiency. Consider tools like personalized coachirg apps or wellness platforms. They analyze your input, your goals, struggles, and successes, and then offer customized feedback to help you progress. Maybe it notices you're more motivated after a morning walk or that your focus wanes on certain days. Based cn these insights, the AI adjusts its prompts, gently encouraging you toward your aspirations.

It's important to recognize AI's limitations. While AI demonstrates impressive capabilities it lacks consciousness and emotional awareness along with moral reasoning abilities. AI lacks true emotional understanding because it analyzes patterns to identify links with various emotional states. AI systems can detect that your speech patterns turn more negative when you are under stress but they do nct experience your stress nor fully understand your personal experience. The system functions as a powerful instrument yet remains a tool that enhances human intuition and compassion.

Knowing AI's capabilities and limitations enables you to apply its tools to boost personal development. AI functions as a reliable ally that strengthens your abilities by revealing hidden elements and providing insights you might miss, along with data-driven advice while you maintain complete control over decisions. The partnership between human cognition and AI analysis creates opportunities for personal discovery and endurance that lead you to achieve your highest potential in today's multifaceted environment (Angel Number 5955 Meaning - Great Opportunities In Life - SunSigns.Org).
AI Milestones: A Comprehensive Look at Artificial Intelligence Evolution.

https://www.cognitech.systems/blog/artificial-intelligence/entry/milestones-in-ai-development

Turing test – Generative AI Commons. https://genaicommons.org/glossary/turing-test/

Exploring the Transformative Power of Artificial Intelligence. https://article.pk/exploring-the-transformative-power-of-artificial-intelligence-745

5 Facts You Don't Know About AI - ChatGPT Was Not the First AI Product - itsaiworld. https://itsaiworld.com/5-facts-you-dont-know-about-ai/

Can Artificial Intelligence Replace Human Intelligence Ppt?. https://www.123articleonline.com/articles/1350740/can-artificial-intelligence-replace-human-intelligence-ppt

(2019). Singapore : NUS deep-learning AI system puts Singapore on the global map of big data analytics. MENA Report

Leveraging AI for Customer Behavior Prediction in Digital Marketing. https://www.rattlewebsolutions.com/post/leveraging-ai-for-customer-behavior-prediction-in-digital-marketing

Angel Number 5955 Meaning - Great Opportunities In Life - SunSigns.Org. https://www.sunsigns.org/angel-number-5955-meaning/

Ch. 2 - Ethical AI: Protecting Privacy and Preserving Humanity

The modern digital era demands more urgent and complex conversations about data privacy. The increasing sophistication of artificial intelligence systems requires substantial personal information for integration into daily life functions. A continuous collection and analysis of personal data takes place through social media platforms and online shopping websites as well as health applications and smart home technologies. AI achieves exceptional performance through this data but simultaneously generates substantial dangers.

A significant security breach occurs at a widely used health-tracking app, resulting in the exposure of sensitive health data to millions of users. This situation exposes people to identity theft and financial fraud while removing their personal control, which makes them defenseless and betraying their trust. The danger exists now as it has already appeared in multiple ways. The 2018 Cambridge Analytica scandal became notorious when millions of Facebook users' data were collected without permission and then leveraged to sway political campaigns. Clearview AI, a facial recognition firm, illegally collected billions of images from the internet, which resulted in widespread international protests due to privacy breaches. The unauthorized use of personal information via artificial intelligence systems undermines public trust and causes actual harm to both people and communities.

AI advancements have caused widespread concern, which has led governments and international bodies to create protective rules for consumers. The European Union implemented the General Data Protection Regulation (GDPR) as a key response in 2018 (Ma, X., Wei, X., Chen, Z., Han, H., & Zhao, J. (2022). ECC: Passenger Counting in the Elevator Using Commodity WiFi. Applied Sciences, 12(14), 7321.). The legislation established new requirements for companies to receive unambiguous and explicit permission before they can collect personal information. The regulation provides users with rights to access their information and to request corrections or deletions while requiring companies to disclose their data handling practices. The adoption of the regulation prompted numerous organizations to update their privacy policies to meet requirements while boosting public understanding of data usage.

California's CCPA became effective in 2020 and provides state residents with the power to both know what data businesses collect about them and to withhold consent for selling their personal information. The CCPA represents an essential move toward regaining control of personal information for individuals, despite having a narrower scope than GDPR. The Personal Information Protection Law (PIPL) of China, enacted in 2021, sets strict data protection rules with a strong focus on consent while placing limitations on data transfers across national borders. The development of new legal structures demonstrates an expanding awareness that privacy should be considered a basic human right instead of an optional privilege.

However, awareness alone isn't enough. People need to actively evaluate their personal information-sharing practices while implementing protective measures for their privacy. People should frequently check their social media privacy options while refraining from sharing excessive personal information online and selecting AI tools that emphasize strong data protection measures. People need to implement practical security measures like activating two-factor authentication and using encrypted messaging services, along with supporting companies that maintain clear data policies to protect their personal information in a world where data functions as a currency.

Pause for a moment and reflect: What level of comfort do you feel when providing data every day? Are you aware of the specific apps and devices that can access your personal information? Do you know what privacy laws grant you as a holder of personal information? The initial action toward becoming a more aware and empowered member of this AI-driven reality begins with asking these questions. Data protection extends beyond avoiding security breaches to maintaining personal autonomy and dignity because personal information represents a fundamental asset in today's society.

Bias in AI Systems:

(Bias in AI refers to the presence of unfair or prejudiced outcomes resulting from skewed or incomplete training data (Bias - SENEN GROUP | Human-Centric Transformations through Data, Analytics & AI). These biases often reflect historical inequalities and can lead to discriminatory decisions in areas like facial recognition, hiring, and lending.)

The growing integration of artificial intelligence into daily activities such as social media feeds and loan approvals creates significant ethical challenges due to the bias present in these systems (What is UnFite? All You Need to Know - UnFite). AI models can achieve objectivity only through unbiased data, although they promise fairness in their design. The data that feeds AI systems usually carries existing societal biases alongside historical prejudices and inequalities.

The expanding application of facial recognition technology by police forces and security organizations has exposed significant biases. Research demonstrates that facial recognition systems more frequently misidentify women and people of color compared to other demographic groups. Error rates for Black women in facial recognition technology can be up to 34%, whereas white males experience error rates of only 1%. The differences found in facial recognition technology extend beyond technical issues because they result in real-world impacts like wrongful arrests and service denial while perpetuating existing social inequalities.

A major tech company discovered that its AI recruitment system consistently showed a preference for male applicants during hiring processes. The AI system adopted gender biases present in historical hiring data during its training process and continued to propagate these patterns. The results show why it is essential to challenge the perceived neutrality of AI systems since algorithms can reflect and intensify human defects despite appearing unbiased.

These biases originate from the training data. (Training data consists of the datasets used to teach an AI system how to make decisions or predictions (Stable diffusion VS Midjourney: All you need to know). If the data contains historical inequalities, the AI system may inadvertently learn and replicate those biases in its outputs.) When AI learns from data that centers on specific groups or mirrors existing societal biases, it will unintentionally continue those biases in its operations. The use of this technology without proper safeguards raises serious ethical concerns about its fairness and justice, as well as the effects it will have on society.

Addressing these issues requires a deliberate approach. Scheduled audits serve as an effective measure to detect biased results and prevent potential harm. AI development relies on training with diverse datasets that encompass all aspects of human experiences to operate effectively. When ethicists, social scientists, and representatives from marginalized communities participate in design and oversight processes, it leads to significant bias reduction. The AI Now Institute and similar organizations work to enhance the representation of diverse voices to guide AI development toward fairness and equity according to societal values.

Reflect on personal experiences with bias. Have you ever faced or observed unfair treatment rooted in stereotypes? Recognize how AI systems might mirror those same biases, often without awareness. Acknowledging this is the first step toward advocating for more ethical, fair, and inclusive AI, an essential pursuit for anyone committed to integrity and societal progress in this technology-driven age.

Establishing Clear Ethical Principles:

Developing explicit ethical guidelines transcends best practices because it becomes an ethical obligation during our journey through AI's fast-changing environment. These principles serve as guiding lights, ensuring that AI aligns with core values: The ethical principles must encompass recognition of human dignity and operational transparency, together with accountability and fairness standards. Ethical principles function as a moral compass to enable us to utilize AI's potential while ensuring protection for our rights and well-being.

Building responsible AI starts with transparency. Consider the application of an artificial intelligence system that analyzes thousands of resumes for candidate selection. The lack of transparency prevents you from comprehending the AI's decision-making process, including the data it examines and factors it values alongside potential biases affecting its judgments. Transparency requires organizations to reveal all operational processes while ensuring they remain comprehensible. Microsoft, IBM, and Google have responded to this requirement by creating ethics boards and guidelines that mandate their teams to share details about algorithm operations and data utilization. Trust grows between users and organizations when transparent practices enable users to make better decisions.

Accountability is equally vital. Who needs to take responsibility when AI systems create harmful results by incorrectly identifying individuals or unfairly denying loans? Ethical frameworks require organizations to take responsibility for their AI systems' effects. The organization must perform routine audits and transparently correct and adjust any discovered biases or defects. Being accountable requires us to accept responsibility for the effects of our creations while actively working to avoid harmful outcomes.

A human-centered approach represents the fundamental principle of responsible AI development. (Human-centered AI is the principle that technology should be designed to enhance human well-being, not replace or diminish it. This approach prioritizes empathy, ethical design, and respect for human dignity.)

The purpose of technology is to assist people rather than

substitute for or reduce their value. Artificial intelligence systems must focus on enhancing human well-being while maintaining the dignity of individuals. AI tools designed to assist with mental health support need to function as supplements to human therapists by delivering valuable insights while preserving essential human relationships.

Practical examples illustrate these principles. The AI Now Institute's 2019 report recommended that AI development teams include ethicists and social scientists to ensure ethical considerations during technology development. Their research demonstrates the critical need for varied viewpoints to uncover and correct biases before AI systems operate in sensitive domains such as criminal justice or financial sectors. Mozilla, among other companies, actively promotes ethical technology principles through open-source development, which focuses on human rights instead of profit generation.

Individuals hold significant power in determining ethical standards. When we evaluate our core beliefs, including questions like "What are my red lines for AI use?" we gain the power to support ethical technology practices. Our decisions to either withdraw support from data-abusing companies or require increased transparency help shape the overall ethical environment.

The creation and adherence to ethical principles extend beyond simple compliance. The purpose is to establish trust while protecting human rights and making sure AI becomes a positive force. Every algorithm contains a human story that should be treated with respect and fairness and granted dignity. Developing responsible AI requires teamwork based on unwavering dedication to fundamental principles that place human needs first.

Ma, X., Wei, X., Chen, Z., Han, H., & Zhao, J. (2022). ECC: Passenger Counting in the Elevator Using Commodity WiFi. Applied Sciences, 12(14), 7321.

Bias - SENEN GROUP | Human-Centric Transformations through Data, Analytics & AI. https://senengroup.com/glossary/bias/

What is UnFite? All You Need to Know - UnFite. https://theunfite.org/

Stable diffusion VS Midjourney: All you need to know. https://www.yeschat.ai/blog-Stable-diffusion-VS-Midjourney-All-you-need-to-know-12491

Ch. 3 - Reimagining Personal Development: A New Framework for Growth

I magine starting your day with an intelligent companion who subtly directs your actions and gains a deeper understanding of you over time. Real-time feedback loops demonstrate transformative power because they represent an innovative approach to personal growth. AI technology enables continuous data processing, which allows people to obtain real-time feedback about their habits and progress. Personal growth develops into an active and reactive path instead of remaining an unreachable target.

Fitness applications such as Fitbit and WHOOP keep track of your physical movement, heartbeat rate, and sleep behavior while giving you daily tailored advice. The app will propose a brief walk or some stretching exercises when it detects reduced activity levels. Poor sleep quality might lead you to modify your evening schedule by adopting earlier screen time limits or meditation sessions. The real-time nudges offer direct advice that helps people transform their theoretical goals into everyday actions.

This principle extends beyond physical health. The young professional Maya works towards developing her emotional resilience. The AI journaling app "Reflectly" provides her with mood insights and coping strategies every evening. During the course of multiple weeks, Maya realized that her emotional stability improved as she practiced mindfulness exercises after stressful meetings. (Mindfulness exercises are short, intentional practices such as breathing techniques or body scans that cultivate focused awareness of the present moment, helping to reduce stress and enhance emotional regulation (Pain Management | Mindset For Change). Body scanning, on the other hand, is the mindfulness technique of body scanning, which requires systematic attention to the body's different parts to achieve physical relaxation and enhanced bodily awareness while developing emotional regulation. Therapists and people working on their personal growth use body scanning as a method to manage stress and ground themselves.) Maya practiced a 5-minute mindful breathing exercise using her AI journaling app after stressful meetings. Starting, she would establish a comfortable seated position while closing her eyes to concentrate entirely on her breath moving in and out of her body. Each time thoughts about the meeting intrude her mind, she calmly guides her focus back to her breathing pattern while avoiding self-judgment.

Her consistent practice of this straightforward exercise builds her emotional control over time which leads to more composed reactions to workplace stressors and an increased capacity to handle emotional challenges. Immediate feedback turns her emotional development into a measurable strategy that she can actively pursue.

Research highlights the significance of immediacy. Research demonstrates that immediate feedback can improve learning outcomes by up to 20%. People who witness immediate outcomes from their actions stay engaged longer and become better at making necessary adjustments to tackle challenges. The experience mirrors that of having a coach who whispers continual guidance and support while you actively work towards your goals.

The importance of immediate reinforcement in habit formation has been recognized by psychologists for many years. BJ Fogg's Behavior Model highlights that successful behavior change depends on three elements: motivation, ability, and a prompt. (BJ Fogg's Behavior Model proposes that behavior change happens when these three elements, motivation, ability, and a timely prompt, converge, enabling the ability to make change easier and more sustainable.) AI functions as the catalyst for AI-supported personal development by delivering timely and mild interventions when change becomes possible. AI provides personalized support by recommending brief mindfulness sessions on busy workdays and gratitude entries after demanding weeks to target significant moments.

(BJ Fogg's Behavior Model proposes that behavior change happens when these three elements, motivation, ability, and a timely prompt, converge, enabling the ability to make change easier and more sustainable.)

The application of this concept reaches into behavioral economics as demonstrated by the Nudge Theory, which was developed by Richard Thaler and Cass Sunstein (Choice Architecture (Behavioural Economics) | Reference Library | Economics | tutor2u). (Nudge Theory, developed by behavioral economists Richard Thaler and Cass Sunstein, suggests that small, well-designed prompts can guide people toward better decisions without limiting their freedom of choice.) Nudges operate as gentle prompts that guide people toward improved decision- making while preserving their ability to choose freely. AI-powered feedback systems embody this principle perfectly: The feedback system provides suggestions for healthier habits and improved routines alongside reflective exercises while maintaining respect for user autonomy and promoting constructive behavior. AI systems deliver tailored suggestions that guide you to your optimal self without direct commands.

AI platforms in personal development monitor real-time data about your mood along with your communication style and decision-making behavior. Sentiment analysis enables mood- tracking apps to monitor daily emotional changes which help you identify stress patterns and activities that boost your mood. Immediate feedback allows you to change your routines or select happier activities while adopting relaxation techniques at the perfect times.

Real-time feedback loops provide instant visibility into growth since they translate development into concrete and immediate experiences. You gain continuous actionable insights rather than waiting weeks for performance reviews or months to observe progress. The never-ending stream of data turns your personal growth journey into an interactive dialogue that develops alongside your personal evolution. Growth happens through consistent small daily changes that build into significant transformation, in addition to achieving major milestones.

Picture yourself sitting silently during early morning hours with a pen ready to record your thoughts about your day and personal challenges. Visualize the act of self-reflection becoming magnified by AI technology, which documents your mental states while providing analysis to facilitate real-time personal development. The power lies in merging deep personal reflection with data analytics capabilities through AI technology. The blend of deep personal reflection with objective analysis produces a dynamic conversation between your internal experience and measurable data.

Advanced AI tools now function as personal guides that enable users to discover previously hidden patterns and insights. Mood-tracking applications use sentiment analysis algorithms to evaluate personal journal entries along with social media updates and voice recordings in order to identify emotional patterns that develop over time. The insights from tracking tools highlight hidden emotional changes like stress fluctuations over time to help you understand your emotional patterns.

For instance, an AI journaling app might detect that feelings of frustration increase after long work hours, prompting you to reconsider your schedule. Alternatively, it may be found that moments of happiness are associated with outdoor walks or social interactions, encouraging you to prioritize those activities. Transforming abstract feelings into concrete data makes your personal growth journey more informed and intentional.

Research supports this approach. Studies show that self-reflection can enhance problem-solving abilities by up to 50%. When combined with data analytics, this process becomes even more effective. Understanding emotional patterns through measurable insights increases self-awareness, enabling better decision- making. You begin to perceive yourself as a complex, evolving system one you can comprehend, nurture, and optimize.

This integration fosters a new kind of conversation: Your personal insights blend with AI's objective analysis to form a powerful partnership. Their collaboration produces a feedback loop which speeds up growth. Through reflection people identify potential improvements while AI insights expand comprehension and point to new directions. You gain access to a compassionate mentor alongside a perceptive analyst who together focuses on helping you reach your personal best.

In practical terms, this approach transforms your emotional awareness into an ongoing dialogue that actively directs your behavior. AI-powered analytics work as a compassionate mirror that provides clear reflections of your inner world when you focus on stress management, building resilience, and enhancing self-understanding. (AI-powered analytics refer to systems that automatically process large amounts of personal data such as journal entries, activity logs, or communication styles to generate personalized insights that support self-awareness and growth). Through this synergy, people gain the ability to make better decisions while adapting faster and establishing a profound self-connection based on genuine introspection and exact comprehension.

The personal development journey undergoes a transformation when AI combines introspection with real-time feedback and behavioral nudging. (Behavioral nudging involves subtle, carefully designed cues or prompts that steer people toward healthier or more beneficial behaviors while preserving their autonomy). AI serves as a complement to human growth and triumph by enhancing our capabilities to become aware, adjust, and flourish through previously unpredictable methods. The collaboration between human wisdom and artificial intelligence launches an innovative phase of personal change characterized by immediate response capabilities and deliberate intention alongside lasting strength.

Pain Management | Mindset For Change.
https://www.mindset-for-change.com/products/pain-management/

Choice Architecture (Behavioural Economics) | Reference Library | Economics | tutor2u. https://www.tutor2u.net/economics/reference/behavioural-economics-choice-architecture

Ch. 4 - Selecting the Right AI Tools for Achieving Your Personal Goals

Y ou find yourself at a junction where your personal aspirations stretch out ahead of you as an endless panorama. Your goals fluctuate between building emotional strength and increasing productivity or mindfulness depending on the day. Meaningful progress depends on selecting tools that align with your goals and enhance your genuine path.

The connection between AI tools and your personal and professional goals transcends mere convenience to establish a synergistic relationship that drives growth. Tools that reflect your aspirations evolve from simple applications into powerful agents of transformation. Reflectly functions as a reflective partner which assists users in building emotional resilience through guided journaling prompts. (Reflectly utilizes artificial intelligence to create a journaling app that supports users in emotional processing through writing prompts provided each day. The system employs machine learning techniques to detect emotional trends and deliver reflections based on mood while delivering customized motivation and insights to bolster both mental health and emotional toughness).

Daylio gives users an uncomplicated yet effective approach to visualizing their emotional patterns while providing essential insights that help them understand their feelings better. (Daylio enables users to document their daily activities and feelings through visual icons and simple text notes. The system creates personalized graphs and statistics over time which demonstrate how specific activities or behaviors impact mood, enabling users to understand their habits' connection to emotional health).

Begin by clearly defining your goals. Write them down in a specific manner. Do you want to manage stress better, improve focus, or cultivate healthier habits? Once your goals are clear, conduct a personal needs assessment. This involves asking focused questions:
• What specific outcome am I seeking?
• What behaviors or habits need to change?
• How much time can I realistically dedicate daily?
• Do I prefer visual feedback, written reflections, or guided prompts?
• Mapping your needs ensures that you choose a tool aligned with both your aspirations and your lifestyle.

Once your goals are clarified, create a visual map or a simple chart linking each objective to potential AI tools.

For example:

Goal	Suggested AI Tool	Notes
Emotional resilience	Reflectly	Journaling prompts for emotional processing
Mood tracking	Daylio	Daily mood and activity logs
Mindfulness	Calm or Headspace	Guided meditation sessions
Habit formation	Habitica	Gamified habit tracking and behavior reinforcement
Productivity boosting	Motion or Reclaim.ai	AI-driven scheduling and time optimization

This structured approach turns ambiguous aspirations into actionable steps, transforming tool selection into a strategic process designed for your needs. As your goals change, review and revise this map to remain in sync with your development.

The true power of aligning goals with the right tools lies in intentionality. When your tools serve your specific dreams, they become partners that support, motivate, and guide you every step of the way. Thoughtfully pairing your aspirations with technology greatly enhances your efforts to achieve genuine, lasting transformation.

Choosing AI tools for personal development requires a careful balance between simple usability and advanced technological features. The equilibrium between tool usability and advanced functionality decides if the tool becomes an effortless part of your daily routine or an overwhelming barrier.

Reflectly utilizes an AI-enabled journaling app that features an easy-to-use interface that enables users to share their thoughts effortlessly (Better communication - better CII management). Just open the app, type, and reflect. Replika stands out as a sophisticated AI platform because it provides comprehensive emotional modeling capabilities, deep conversation options, and user-customizable avatars. (Replika operates as a conversational AI chatbot with the capability to simulate empathetic dialogue and provide emotional companionship. Through its interactions the program adjusts its tone and responses which results in a customized user experience. Replika serves as a platform for users who seek emotional support and self-reflection without fear of judgment. The platform incorporates mood recognition technology alongside options for personalized avatar creation). The powerful attributes of these features will impress users, but they can become overwhelming for those who prefer simple options.

Why does this matter? Advanced tools require users to grasp more complex functionalities, which increases the difficulty of initial learning. Sophisticated features provide substantial advantages through emotional analytics and personal coaching yet require user comfort with their navigation to be effective. (AI-driven emotional analytics processes data from journal entries and voice recordings as well as usage patterns to track emotional states across time. By analyzing mood fluctuations and stress triggers along with well-being patterns, these tools give users the power to make better mental health decisions). Beginners often become frustrated, lose interest, or stop using complex systems altogether.

To find the right balance, consider these factors:
• User interface: Is the platform clean, straightforward, and easy to navigate? Does it avoid unnecessary steps?
• Accessibility: Can you access the tool across your devices, smartphone, tablet, or computer with minimal setup?
• Support and resources: Does the provider offer tutorials, FAQs, or responsive support?

As a marketing professional with limited time Sarah attempted to use an advanced goal-tracking application featuring multiple integrations but she found the platform too complex. By choosing the simple Daylio app for quick mood and activity entries through minimal taps she became more engaged and consistent. She could use the app in her everyday schedule effortlessly thanks to its straightforward design.

Test various tools before settling on one. Many offer free versions or trial periods; use these to assess your comfort. Ask yourself:
• Do I find this intuitive?
• Can I see myself using it regularly without frustration?

If not, explore alternatives better suited to your comfort level.

Remember, a highly sophisticated tool isn't necessarily better. The most effective choice is the one you will actually use consistently. Prioritize your comfort and confidence, and avoid being swayed solely by features that may exceed your needs or capabilities at this stage.

Choosing an AI tool that suits your ease of use ensures your personal growth journey is sustainable and enjoyable. Empower yourself with technology that enhances your progress, rather than creates barriers.

For AI tools to genuinely support personal growth, they must become part of your daily routines. When seamlessly integrated, these tools can continuously help you achieve your goals instead of becoming burdensome or forgotten. Accomplishing this requires thoughtful planning and a readiness to adapt. Find times throughout your day when your mind is open to reflection or transformation, which include morning routines and evening wind downs as well as commutes and lunch breaks. The best moments for naturally integrating AI tools into your routine occur during these times. By creating a daily prompt to launch a journaling application such as Reflectly alongside your morning coffee routine, you can transform basic journaling into a purposeful practice. During lunch breaks, you can use Daylio to track your mood through AI capabilities, which record your emotional state as it happens without interrupting your tasks.

Limited time, forgetfulness, and resistance to change emerge as common obstacles in this process. Overcome these by planning strategically. The first step involves pinpointing distinct times when engagement appears manageable. Establish regular routines that take only five minutes each night to go over insights or set weekly reminders to evaluate your progress. Maintain flexibility by moving your schedule when needed, and focus on identifying new opportunities without feeling guilty.

To develop your unique plan you should chart your daily schedules and determine when these tools will be most beneficial during activities such as your morning meditation practice or your commute time. Determine the specific times and methods for using each tool and establish achievable expectations. Instead of striving for perfection you should pursue consistent use of habits which promote growth without becoming overwhelming.

AI technology progresses at a fast pace, which means the most advanced tools can eventually become obsolete or stop matching your requirements. When this occurs, adaptability becomes critical. Periodically reassess the tools you use.

Ask yourself:
• Does this tool continue to support my progress toward my goals?
• Has my personal focus shifted?
• Do better-suited tools exist for my present path?

Remember, routines and needs evolve over time. Continually evaluate your strategy to implement changes when your objectives change or when new tools become available. The continuous transformation process enables AI to function as a dependable partner that remains unseen yet provides powerful daily guidance for your development.

Create your AI integration strategy by laying out your everyday activities to find the best moments for implementation. An AI integration strategy represents a personalized roadmap detailing the specific steps and timelines for adding AI tools into everyday activities. The strategy requires users to select appropriate tools and find regular usage times, such as morning routines or evening wind-downs, to support specific objectives like emotional resilience, focus, and productivity. Your growth influences the strategy, which maintains its effectiveness and relevance over time. Mark down three specific times during your day, including morning hours, midday periods, and evening time. Determine the tools for use as well as define the specific actions you will perform and the time investment required. For example, the morning schedule includes five minutes with Reflectly for intention journaling, while the evening involves a review of mood patterns using Daylio before bedtime.

Follow your schedule for one week while tracking successful elements and recognizing spots that need changes. Through this personalized approach, your AI tools will integrate into your daily life and become a consistent ally for your personal development.

Supplemental Details:

Calm and Headspace

Calm and Headspace offer mindfulness and meditation services through artificial intelligence, which tailors sessions according to individual user activity patterns and objectives. The application provides customized guided meditation sessions, breathing techniques and sleep support functionalities which help users to manage stress levels while enhancing focus and mental clarity.

Habitica

Habitica functions as a habit-building productivity app that employs gamification by applying game elements to make behavior modification more engaging. Through virtual rewards and avatar development, users accomplish personal goals while maintaining daily progress streaks and experiencing self- improvement tasks in an interactive way.

Emotional Modeling

Advanced AI systems employ emotional modeling to replicate human emotional understanding. Systems analyze user text and behavioral patterns alongside tone to deliver responses that seem empathetic by predicting emotional states. Emotional modeling enables AI to deliver feedback that seems emotionally aware and contextually suitable, even though AI lacks true consciousness.

AI-Driven Scheduling

Motion and Reclaim.ai represent AI-driven scheduling tools which employ machine learning algorithms to automate calendar management tasks. These platforms analyze your meetings, deadlines, habits, and productivity patterns to automatically schedule tasks during optimal time slots which helps decrease cognitive load while enhancing time management without needing continuous manual input.

Better communication - better CII management. https://www.ankeri.net/post/better-communication-better-cii-management

Ch. 5 - Deepening Emotional Clarity Through AI-Powered Journaling

T hrough *sentiment analysis** we gain transformative insight into our emotional world. The software uses sophisticated artificial intelligence techniques to evaluate the emotional undertone within our language. This technology may act like a reflective surface in journaling by revealing hidden insights from our inner world that stay buried within our everyday thoughts and emotions.

Every morning, you could start by using your digital journal to release your thoughts, frustrations, and hopes while expressing gratitude. The AI technology reads your written entries to determine if they express positive emotions, negative emotions, or neutral expressions. The analytical process reveals patterns over time, which may show mood declines after specific discussions or enhanced gratitude following particular actions. The analysis turns your journaling practice into a continuous personal conversation, which enhances self-understanding with every new entry.

Someone may express their day's stress by writing about feelings of being overwhelmed and frustrated. The AI software recognizes negative emotions in text analysis and then highlights them so users can engage in reflective thinking. As time passes, you might notice that your mood goes down after interacting with certain team members or during periods of intensive work. By identifying these patterns, you gain the ability to take proactive steps to control your emotions through alternative preparation methods or by planning self-care throughout vulnerable periods.

The combination of AI-enhanced journaling with emotional regulation techniques intensifies these benefits. *The Process Model of Emotion Regulation proposed by James Gross** demonstrates that emotional regulation can occur through multiple stages, including situation modification, attention adjustment, and changes in cognitive interpretation (Zhou, S., Wu, Y., & Xu, X. (2023). Linking Cognitive Reappraisal and Expressive Suppression to Mindfulness: A Three-Level Meta-Analysis. *International Journal of Environmental Research and Public Health*, 20(2), 1241.. Journaling, enhanced by AI, naturally supports this process: Journaling backed by AI allows users to spot emotional triggers sooner (situation selection), gain insights that redirect attention (attention deployment), and collect data that supports cognitive reinterpretation of stressful events (cognitive change). AI-enhanced journaling can support emotion regulation practices and promote greater emotional awareness, complementing but not replacing professional therapy.

Research supports the effectiveness of this approach. Reflectly's research demonstrated that their AI-powered journaling platform leads users to gain improved emotional understanding and self-awareness. Through its prompts and feedback mechanism, the app has turned journaling into an active process that has led users to investigate their emotions more deeply. A multitude of users discovered that this technique assisted them in revealing emotional triggers that had escaped their attention before and led them to develop stronger control and resilience.

Sentiment analysis provides a method for extended monitoring of emotional fluctuations. Graphs and charts visualized on dashboards present mood changes which reveal subtle emotional shifts through tangible representations. People often find that their mood gets better when they exercise or do creative activities but gets worse during tough workweeks. Visual insights function as directional tools that lead us to establish better habits and achieve emotional stability.

Emerging technologies are further revolutionizing the journaling landscape. Voice sentiment analysis, *for example, uses AI to evaluate the emotional tone of spoken journal entries. Tools like Jour or Mindsera* now offer options to record audio reflections, detecting stress, calmness, excitement, or sadness based on vocal tone, pacing, and inflection. This provides a more nuanced emotional profile, capturing not just what is said but how it is said. Such capabilities bring emotional awareness even closer to real-time, offering deeper, multimodal perspectives* on our inner world.

Imagine narrating your thoughts aloud after a difficult day — your voice quivers slightly, your pace quickens when discussing work stress, and your tone softens when speaking about family. An AI tool captures these subtleties, providing you with a visualization of emotional peaks and valleys directly linked to your speech. Over time, this enables a more precise understanding of emotional triggers, resilience points, and hidden patterns in emotional expression.

Practical journaling exercises can also enhance the emotional clarity that AI tools facilitate. Consider incorporating daily prompts such as:

• "What was the emotional high point of my day?"
• "When did I feel most challenged today, and what thoughts accompanied it?"
• "What patterns am I beginning to notice about how I handle stress?"
• "Which small action today made me feel proud, connected, or peaceful?"

AI helps by examining journal entries connected to these prompts and revealing themes and emotional patterns that you might not have noticed yourself. Small reflections accumulate over time to form a detailed emotional map that helps you develop healthier habits while deepening your self-knowledge and building stronger resilience.

The ability of AI systems to recognize cognitive patterns* serves as another critical transformation of AI-enhanced journaling. You write in your journal about your thoughts and feelings while an intelligent companion listens quietly and marks the recurring patterns and beliefs that influence your emotions. AI-driven cognitive pattern recognition holds transformative power. The system actively analyzes your entries to discover hidden thought loops that affect your emotions rather than simply recording them. During a week of utilizing an AI-driven journaling application, users begin to identify patterns such as their inclination to catastrophize under stress or a persistent feeling of inadequacy following specific social interactions. The algorithms process your language and tone along with word frequency to detect these patterns, which provide insights that could easily be missed. During overwhelmed days, people tend to use absolutes like "never" or "always," which points to Overgeneralization, a common *cognitive distortion**. Identifying these patterns represents an essential move toward personal transformation.

Scientific studies of cognitive behavioral therapy* back up this strategy. Awareness of negative thinking patterns enables people to challenge and reframe those thoughts, which builds stronger emotional resilience. The use of AI in journaling creates a pathway that connects emotional awareness with cognitive transformation. This tool enables users to monitor their feelings while gaining insight into the underlying beliefs that generate these emotions.

The transformation process turns journaling into an active introspective dialogue based on data-driven insights rather than passive documentation of everyday happenings. Users who notice patterns like constant self-criticism or avoidance behaviors can actively dispute these thoughts to establish healthier ways of thinking. This method gradually develops self-awareness while building emotional flexibility and strength.

Individuals unlock powerful growth opportunities by utilizing AI tools to detect cognitive patterns. Their comprehension evolves from basic awareness to an intricate comprehension of personal stories. The core foundation of meaningful change emerges from awareness, which breaks destructive patterns while establishing a mindset focused on compassion and clarity for growth. Users who maintain regular practice develop stronger *emotional intelligence**ß and resilience, which can enable them to face life challenges with self-assuredness and elegance.

The integration of sentiment analysis with voice recognition and cognitive patterning transforms journaling into an interactive conversation that combines personal reflection with data-driven insights. These tools serve not to replace personal insight but to sharpen it: Sentiment analysis and voice recognition help people discover what they've missed and validate their silent achievements while also pointing out hidden paths to emotional growth. AI serves as a gentle partner during self-reflection, which transforms emotional clarity into both an attainable goal and a sustainable advantage amidst life's intricacies.

Supplemental Details:

Sentiment Analysis

Sentiment analysis represents an AI method that deciphers emotional expressions present in both written and spoken communications. AI uses patterns in word choice along with sentence structure and context to determine whether entries express positive, negative, or neutral emotions. Sentiment analysis operates as a reflective tool in personal development that enables users to achieve enhanced clarity about their emotional changes over time.

Process Model of Emotion Regulation (James Gross)

Psychologist James Gross developed the Process Model of Emotion Regulation which teaches people how to control their emotions through interventions at multiple stages of an emotional reaction. The model identifies several emotion regulation strategies such as altering situations to influence emotional responses along with redirecting attention from unpleasant stimuli and changing perception through cognitive reframing. AI-supported journaling fits seamlessly into the model by assisting users in identifying their emotional triggers while also shifting their attention and reinterpreting their emotional experiences.

Jour*

Jour is an application that uses AI to guide users through

structured journaling practices that aid their emotional wellness by encouraging self-reflection. The service provides its users with an array of therapeutic writing prompts sorted by themes, which include gratitude practices as well as tools for anxiety management and, emotional processing and goal setting exercises. Users can systematically explore their thoughts and emotions through a platform that merges conventional journaling methods with AI-powered mood analysis and insights. The platform enables users to perform brief, regular reflections that make emotional self-awareness a manageable daily routine instead of a burdensome task.

Mindsera*

Mindsera functions as a digital journaling platform that uses artificial intelligence to aid users in developing their mindset while building emotional resilience and leadership skills. Mindsera sets itself apart from simple journaling apps by utilizing AI to evaluate journal entries for patterns in cognition and emotional expressions alongside self-limiting beliefs. The platform delivers visual mind maps together with mental model recommendations and reflective feedback, which converts traditional journaling into a structured means of cognitive and emotional enhancement. Mindsera assists users in emotional processing while enhancing their decision-making skills as well as strategic thinking and emotional intelligence with continuous use.

Situation Selection, Attention Deployment, and Cognitive Change

• Situation Selection*: Select environments and activities or associate with people that enhance your emotional well-being. Individuals can manage their emotional experiences by skipping stressful meetings whenever possible and selecting calming activities to enhance their mood.

- Attention Deployment*: The attention deployment strategy involves directing emotional attention toward or distancing awareness from designated emotional stimuli. Directing attention toward gratitude instead of ruminating on negative events.

- Cognitive Change*: Changing how you interpret an event modifies its emotional effect by seeing a setback as a chance to grow instead of a defeat.

Voice Sentiment Analysis*

Traditional sentiment analysis broadens its scope through voice sentiment analysis which assesses both the spoken content and the method of delivery. By examining vocal elements including tone, pace, volume and inflection AI systems identify emotional cues that show stress excitement sadness or calmness. Using multimodal analysis creates a real-time emotional insight that uncovers complex feelings which traditional text analysis cannot detect.

Journaling Prompts*

Focused questions or statements in journaling prompts act as guides which help users achieve profound self-reflection and emotional understanding. Users benefit from prompts that guide their reflections toward specific themes instead of facing a blank page, which helps them examine moments of joy or stress and recognize achievements while creating a structured reflective process.

Cognitive Pattern Recognition (AI-Driven)*

Artificial intelligence-driven cognitive pattern recognition involves scanning journal entries to detect repeated thought sequences and emotional patterns along with cognitive distortions. AI detects language patterns like frequent negative expressions or exaggerated emotional terms which show mental habits affecting emotional health so users can intentionally work toward better thinking patterns.

Cognitive Distortions (e.g., Overgeneralization)*

Cognitive distortions represent repetitive thought patterns that warp reality and tend to intensify negative emotional experiences. People often experience cognitive distortions, which include overgeneralizing situations (like thinking "I always fail"), catastrophizing outcomes (expecting the worst possible results), and black-and-white thinking (viewing situations as completely good or completely bad). Identifying these cognitive patterns enables people to build emotional resilience through the process of questioning and transforming irrational beliefs.

Cognitive Behavioral Therapy (CBT)*

Cognitive Behavioral Therapy (CBT) represents a scientifically supported psychological treatment that aims to modify dysfunctional thoughts and behaviors to enhance emotional well-being (Therapy for Anxiety in Dallas TX 75204). The method trains people to recognize distorted thoughts and challenge negative assumptions while developing balanced and constructive viewpoints. AI-based journaling platforms function similarly to CBT methods by assisting users in identifying and modifying their emotional thought patterns.

Emotional Intelligence*

Emotional intelligence represents the capacity to perceive and control personal emotions together with understanding and directing other people's feelings. The components of emotional intelligence include self-awareness along with emotional regulation and empathy while also incorporating social skills. Personal development demands building emotional intelligence because it helps individuals face challenges with resilience and compassion.

Multimodal Perspectives*

Through the combination of written text and vocal tone data, multimodal perspectives enable a deeper understanding of a person's emotions. AI systems achieve enhanced emotional profiles for users by analyzing both language and speech together rather than text or voice individually.

Zhou, S., Wu, Y., & Xu, X. (2023). Linking Cognitive Reappraisal and Expressive Suppression to Mindfulness: A Three-Level Meta-Analysis. *International Journal of Environmental Research and Public Health*, 20(2), 1241. https://doi.org/10.3390/ijerph20021241

Therapy for Anxiety in Dallas TX 75204: Bright Space is Here to Help. https://brightspacetherapy.com/therapy-for-anxiety

Ch. 6 - Building Mindfulness Through Adaptive AI Support: A Path to Inner Calm

E nvision an app like Calm or Headspace that truly grasps your emotions as they happen. These meditation guides function as intelligent companions that adapt sessions according to your emotional state rather than remaining generic guides. AI technology enables these applications to examine your meditation duration, feelings before and after sessions, and subtle interaction patterns to generate personalized experiences for you. When you often feel anxious before meditating, the app recommends a calming body scan or a gentle breathing exercise to ease your mind. During a body scan mindfulness meditation practice participants move their attention systematically through each body part starting at the head and proceeding to the feet or vice versa. The objective is to notice bodily sensations, including tension, warmth, and relaxation, without trying to alter them through nonjudgmental acceptance.

The app logs your reported relief or increased mindfulness after a session to customize subsequent recommendations. The personalized feedback loop boosts both engagement levels and session relevance for users. A thorough understanding of stress physiology helps reveal how AI can transform mindfulness practices. The human stress response known as "fight, flight, or freeze" developed through evolution to protect our ancestors from immediate dangers. Danger triggers the body to release cortisol and adrenaline, which increases heart rate while enhancing mental focus and muscle readiness. The stress response saves lives during emergencies but frequently malfunctions in current times by triggering everyday stressors like traffic jams and work pressures. Continuous activation of this stress reaction produces anxiety symptoms and emotional fatigue while diminishing mindfulness capacity.

AI-powered mindfulness tools *monitor physiological indicators such as increased heart rates and tense muscles to enable people to detect stress onset before it grows worse. Real-time intervention suggestions from emotion-responsive meditation apps* allow people to address stress early on while developing a sense of calm before feelings of overwhelm become established.

The research underscores the impact of tailored approaches. People who use emotion-responsive meditation apps experience higher levels of contentment and stronger emotional ties. Participants using AI-enhanced tools demonstrated 30% higher mindfulness score improvements than traditional app users, according to 2022 research findings. The apps send reminders to users to meditate during stressful situations based on detected stress patterns, such as challenging afternoon meetings or long workdays. The intelligent schedule feature makes meditation a daily routine which elevates it from a sporadic practice to a fundamental daily activity.

Through AI-driven personalization, these apps not only act as meditation guides but also help users explore their emotional states more thoroughly. These tools act as gentle companions who respond to your current state while aiding you in developing a sustainable mindfulness routine that adapts to your changing needs. This technology helps you develop emotional understanding and resilience, which turns mindfulness into a continuous path of self-knowledge throughout your life.

AI-driven systems perform well in habit analysis and delivering personalized recommendations. An AI app detects late afternoon stress patterns over multiple weeks and suggests a quick five-minute mindfulness exercise for that time. These insights are uniquely designed for you using your personal data to help integrate your routine seamlessly into your daily life.

Progress tracking alongside reminders serves as the foundation for establishing durable habits. An AI assistant might send a gentle notification at your preferred time, say 3:30 p.m. At your chosen time of 3:30 p.m., you will receive a friendly reminder to stop for a moment to take deep breaths while reconnecting with yourself. The AI system analyzes your session logs to identify the most effective techniques for you and refines its recommendations to boost your emotional resilience and clarity.

To get the most out of this technology, you should practice exercises that are practical in nature. Build a mindfulness routine tailored to your needs with AI suggestions including a 10-minute breathing exercise after lunchtime and a grounding technique during your travel to work. Maintain a log to track the effects of each mindfulness practice on your emotional state and concentration. Reflect on your experiences regularly to determine the most effective routine elements and make necessary changes. Through continuous practice, your mindfulness routine becomes a stable element of your everyday existence.

Implementing AI into your daily practices helps establish regular patterns and personal development. The technology serves as a supportive guide that leads you to enhanced self-understanding and emotional harmony. As your practice deepens, mindfulness becomes not just an occasional effort but an intrinsic, enriching part of who you are. Thoughtful, compassion-driven technology assists you in maintaining an ongoing process of self-discovery.

The development of mindfulness technology will progress towards predictive mindfulness* because AI systems will learn to identify optimal moments for mindfulness interventions. Predictive AI models enable proactive mindfulness practice recommendations by analyzing behavior patterns alongside physiological and historical stress response data.

Imagine an AI app that recognizes subtle changes in your behavior: Behavioral indicators such as faster typing speed together with an increase in smartphone usage and reduced concentration duration suggest emerging stress. The application softly prompts you to perform a breathing exercise prior to your stress levels rising. Predictive AI systems can identify early signs of emotional dysregulation through heart rate variability* alongside movement patterns and interaction data before providing micro- interventions to stop emotional spirals from happening.

Such anticipatory approaches are already being explored in the health and wellness domains. Early prototypes of wearable technologies can predict when a user may need hydration, rest, or movement based on bio-signals. Extending this to mindfulness practices represents a profound shift from reactive management to proactive emotional optimization. In this future, AI doesn't just respond to who you are in the moment; it helps shape the conditions for your most mindful, centered self.

Biofeedback Integration:

Visualize yourself in your preferred peaceful spot, which can be your home's snug nook or a serene park, as you prepare to enhance your mindfulness practice. Envision a calm yet intelligent companion who observes your physical cues to steer you through stress relief and relaxation with precision. The fusion of biofeedback technology with artificial intelligence creates a groundbreaking partnership that transforms physiological readings into significant insights and strengthens your bond with your internal state.

Personalization makes biofeedback, combined with AI technology, so effective.During meditation or breathing exercises, the AI continuously monitors heart rate variability along with skin temperature and breathing patterns. When heart rate readings show stress signs, the system recommends relaxation methods such as fast breathing exercises or body scanning for calm restoration.

Research emphasizes the effectiveness of this integration. Research reveals that biofeedback improves mindfulness by delivering real-time data about mental and emotional conditions. Observing your heart rate slow down and breathing stabilize gives you control over your emotional state. Real-time awareness enhances emotional control, which turns mindfulness into active self-empowerment instead of passive watching.

Imagine a person who starts using a biofeedback-enabled meditation app at the beginning of the year. People find it challenging to sustain concentration and experience feelings of being overwhelmed at first. As the application monitors users' physiological data over time it detects patterns like elevated heart rates during stressful events and generates personalized advice. After several weeks they observe decreased baseline stress levels along with enhanced resilience and better emotional management confidence.

Personalization makes biofeedback, combined with AI technology, so effective. The system adjusts to your feedback by delivering customized guidance that develops alongside your journey. This technology serves as a compassionate coach to help you reach your goals of anxiety reduction, emotional clarity, and present-moment awareness by listening and learning from you and guiding you along your journey.

Using biofeedback in your daily routine requires wearing a small device while practicing regularly to achieve targets like reducing your resting heart rate and keeping your breathing consistent. The AI monitors your development while celebrating your milestones and promoting continued commitment. These brief interventions, which are conducted over time, develop an adaptable mind that handles life's stressful situations gracefully.

Through the combination of biofeedback and AI technology, mindfulness evolves from a passive undertaking into a dynamic conversation between the body and mind. Through its methods, the system connects conscious awareness to practical actions, thus enabling people to control their emotions in a manageable way. Developing this skill enables you to build confidence in your capability to respond thoughtfully during chaotic situations. This embodies the future of mindful living: personalized, responsive, and profoundly transformative.

Benefits of a Body Scan:

• Stress and Anxiety Reduction:
• Body scans promote relaxation by activating the parasympathetic nervous system*, which counteracts the body's stress response (Creswell et al., 2016) (The Impact of Stress on the Body and the Role of Bowen Technique in Relief - Written by Adam Lison).
• Improved Mind-Body Awareness:
• Enhances an individual's sensitivity to internal bodily states (interoception*), leading to better emotional regulation and early

recognition of stress signals (Mehling et al., 2011).

• Pain Management:

• Studies show that consistent practice can decrease the subjective experience of chronic pain by changing how pain is processed and perceived in the brain (Kabat-Zinn, 1982) (Understanding Alternative Therapies for Managing Chronic Pain).

• Enhanced Sleep Quality:

• Practicing body scans before bedtime has been linked to improvements in falling asleep faster and staying asleep longer (Ong et al., 2014).

Supplementary detail(s)*

AI-Powered Mindfulness Tools*

Digital platforms known as AI-powered mindfulness tools leverage artificial intelligence to tailor meditation and mental health experiences to individual users. The adaptive guidance provided by these tools is based on analyzed data from user usage patterns, together with self-reported emotions and biometric signals like heart rate, to match the user's present emotional or cognitive needs. AI mindfulness tools continuously adapt based on user behavior and stress patterns to provide relevant interventions instead of static, uniform sessions.

Emotion-Responsive Meditation Apps*

This class of mindfulness technology contains emotion-responsive meditation apps that modify their responses instantly according to the emotional state of the user. The apps detect heightened stress levels to suggest calming breathing sessions while they analyze low mood indicators to propose energizing mindfulness activities. The operation of these applications depends on either direct emotional feedback from users or indirect mood interpretation through interaction data and analysis of information from wearable devices and vocal tone detection. Users receive a meditation experience tailored to their emotional state, which provides personal and relevant mindfulness support.

Predictive Mindfulness (Predictive AI Models)*

Predictive mindfulness uses artificial intelligence to foresee users' emotional and physiological requirements prior to the full onset of stress or anxiety. Predictive AI models use behavioral patterns alongside historical emotional responses and wearable sensor data as well as environmental signals like calendar events and time of day to determine when users become vulnerable. Through the use of predictive micro-interventions like calming prompts or breathing cues these systems work to stop emotional dysregulation before it starts. Digital mental health care has evolved substantially through its shift from reactive support methods to anticipatory support mechanisms.

Biofeedback Technology*

Biofeedback systems measure and display live physiological data, including heart rate and breathing patterns, to assist users in managing their physical and emotional responses. Biofeedback which began as a clinical therapy tool has become available through wearable devices and smartphone applications. AI integration with biofeedback creates intelligent systems that recognize stress indicators and recommend specific mindfulness exercises. The combination of body data and machine insight enables people to understand their stress responses better and implement effective management techniques.

Heart Rate Variability (HRV)*

Heart Rate Variability (HRV) measures the fluctuation in intervals between consecutive heartbeats (Alonso-Pérez-Chao, E., Calleja-

González, J., Jiménez Sáiz, S., & Jiménez Sáiz, S., 2024). Heart Rate Variability in Basketball: The Golden Nugget of Holistic Adaptation? Applied Sciences, 14(21), 10013). A healthy heart displays minor variations that correspond to breathing patterns as well as stress and emotional stimuli. High HRV typically signifies effective physical fitness levels and emotional control, along with strong stress resistance, but low HRV suggests possible fatigue or ongoing stress. Mindfulness tools enhanced with AI capabilities track HRV to identify signs of emotional overload early and provide soothing interventions to address them.

Parasympathetic Nervous System*

The body uses its autonomic nervous system's parasympathetic branch to manage restful functions and digestion. The parasympathetic system reduces cardiac activity while lowering blood pressure and encourages digestive function and stress recovery. The activation of the parasympathetic system produces states of calmness and balance which makes it an essential biological focus for mindfulness techniques. Deep breathing alongside body scanning and meditation practices activate this system to provide an antidote to the "fight, flight, or freeze" reaction.

Interoception*

Interoception refers to bodily internal state awareness, which enables recognition of physical sensations like heartbeat and breathing, along with hunger and tension. People who possess heightened interoceptive awareness can identify early emotional shifts, such as recognizing stress buildup before it becomes overwhelming. Body scanning through mindfulness practices develops interoception, which becomes an effective tool for emotional control and resilience when AI and biofeedback enhancements are applied.

The Impact of Stress on the Body and the Role of Bowen Technique in Relief - Written by Adam Lison. https://www.devonbowenclinic.co.uk/post/the-impact-of-stress-on-the-body-and-the-role-of-bowen-technique-in-relief-written-by-adam-lison

Understanding Alternative Therapies for Managing Chronic Pain https://tranquilhealthnews.com/understanding-alternative-therapies-for-managing-chronic-pain/

Alonso-Pérez-Chao, E., Calleja-González, J., Jiménez Sáiz, S., & Jiménez Sáiz, S. (2024). Heart Rate Variability in Basketball: The Golden Nugget of Holistic Adaptation? Applied Sciences, 14(21), 10013.

Ch. 7 - Enhancing Resilience Through AI-Assisted Coaching

Y ou wake up on Monday morning and immediately feel overwhelmed before even rising from your bed. Anxiety flutters across your mind whenever you think about upcoming deadlines or upcoming difficult conversations. Your personal resilience map uses emotional triggers as guiding signposts. Suppose you developed the ability to recognize these triggers with complete clarity and precision? By understanding the patterns in your emotional responses you can leverage this knowledge to develop stronger resilience.

This is where emotional trigger mapping *becomes a powerful tool, especially when combined with AI. Previously, recognizing triggers depended on self-awareness and memory, often leading to incomplete or biased insights. Now, AI-driven platforms like BetterUp* analyze your journal entries, interactions, and physiological data, if available, to identify recurring themes and responses. For example, if you record daily reflections or use a coaching app regularly, the AI can detect patterns, perhaps noting that frustration tends to surface during Wednesday meetings or that irritability spikes after certain interactions.

After mapping occurs, these triggers evolve from abstract emotions into concrete data points that enable you to observe them, analyze them, and take action. Understanding that you typically react emotionally to criticism after exhausting workdays allows you to plan proactive coping strategies beforehand, which include taking a brief walk, breathing deeply, or reframing your thoughts to handle triggers effectively. The objective is to move from spontaneous responses to planned emotional handling, which requires identifying your triggers and responding positively.

The development of resilience through AI coaching incorporates psychological principles, including grit* and a growth mindset. The term grit describes ongoing dedication and persistent effort toward long-term objectives despite encountering obstacles. Psychologist Angela Duckworth introduced grit as the concept that sustained effort over time matters more than temporary motivation or natural ability. Studies demonstrate that individuals with grit achieve more in academics and their careers and experience greater personal prosperity through demonstrated resilience and sustained psychological health.

For example, aspiring entrepreneur Alex uses an AI coaching tool to set goals while tracking progress and receiving motivational prompts. The daily reinforcement helps him build stronger perseverance, which enables him to overcome early setbacks and eventually reach his goals.

Angela Duckworth describes grit as continuous passion and perseverance directed toward long-term ambitions despite facing difficulties. AI coaching platforms assist in building grit by enabling users to establish specific goals and monitor their incremental achievements while also reminding them of their previous successes to boost confidence in challenging times. The ongoing support through reinforcement builds perseverance while developing resilience when confronting obstacles.

AI-assisted coaching strategies center around Carol Dweck's concept of a Growth Mindset* which states that intelligence and abilities can expand through dedication and effort (Successful Lives Primary Programme: Growth Mindset – Focus Education). The growth mindset involves the understanding that one's abilities and talents can be developed through persistent effort and learning. Psychologist Carol Dweck introduced this perspective to challenge the fixed mindset which considers traits as unchangeable. Studies demonstrate that people who adopt a growth mindset build stronger resilience while achieving better academic and professional results and reacting more positively to challenges.

When users face slow progress the AI coaching app reframes the experience as a natural learning curve component while reminding them about their cumulative growth instead of focusing on immediate results. The reinforcement enables individuals to maintain their motivation and ability to adapt throughout their journey. AI systems teach users to view obstacles as learning experiences instead of failures through constructive reframing methods. An AI system can detect repeated expressions of frustration about slow progress in journal entries and respond with supportive messages such as "Growth is not always visible day-to-day." Here's evidence of your cumulative improvement." The approach develops an attitude where individuals naturally respond with persistence and flexibility.

Regular practice of this process, including trigger detection and root analysis, followed by mindful responses, builds a strong mindset based on self-awareness. Through continuous learning from these insights, you develop the ability to handle setbacks with greater ease while turning emotional vulnerabilities into strengths. AI develops your intuitive understanding by delivering precise self-insights, which strengthens your confidence and allows you to respond well during tough situations. Envision a mental health assistant designed to support you by responding during intense emotions and proactively predicting challenges so you can prepare in advance. Predictive analytics* in mental health now holds the potential to transform mental health care through AI technology. This technology examines extensive personal data sources, including journal entries and mood logs, to identify subtle signals that would typically remain undetected.

AI detects a pattern when an individual records stress during the month's final week and sends alerts about potential upcoming stress while proposing preventive coping techniques. The system suggests calming breathing exercises and mindfulness practices to be completed right before the stressful period starts. The goal is to transform how we deal with stress by moving from only responding to it after it happens to actively predicting and stopping it before it starts.

People develop resilience through this proactive method because it provides them more control over their emotional states. Users receive customized insights and proactive strategies to avoid being taken off guard by emotional lows. People can prepare themselves beforehand to diminish negative emotions and sustain emotional balance.

Platforms like BetterUp and newer AI mental health apps like Spring Health and Wysa* already integrate early-stage predictive analytics, offering personalized mental fitness plans based on user-reported data and biometric trends. As these systems evolve, incorporating data from wearables, daily journals, and digital behaviors, their ability to forecast emotional needs will become increasingly precise. Predictive mental health analytics changes resilience from a reactive survival method into a proactive strength-development process. AI insights enable us to achieve emotional stability as a concrete outcome through strategic foresight and self-awareness.

Waking up to an AI assistant that presents an analysis of your past week's emotional patterns becomes a reality for mental health enhancement. It functions as an active partner, providing customized strategies at the exact moments they are needed. AI platforms deliver personalized coping strategies* that adapt to your unique emotional needs through an individualized approach. When you have increased anxiety during social events such as meetings or group gatherings, AI identifies this behavior by examining your journal entries and mood logs alongside your interactions within coaching tools like BetterUp. This data could recommend precise methods, including breathing exercises and visualization practices, along with mindfulness prompts to soothe your nervous system. Personalized interventions match your triggers and preferences, which leads to higher effectiveness and seamless integration into everyday routines.

Sarah works as a marketing manager in New York City and regularly experiences feelings of being overwhelmed when she needs to present. The AI coaching platform tracks her anxiety symptoms through weekly monitoring of rapid heartbeats and racing thoughts while noticing avoidance of preparation tasks and suggests specific exercises like diaphragmatic breathing and success visualization. Sarah experiences less anxiety and greater confidence in her presentations after regularly practicing recommended micro-interventions.

Personalized coping strategies provide adaptive techniques specifically designed for an individual through analysis of their unique emotional patterns, as well as their lifestyle habits, stress responses, and personal goals.

These well-timed small-scale approaches promote sustainable resilience through natural processes. The consistent application of these targeted micro-practices results in enduring improvements in emotional flexibility and adaptability along with self-regulation skills.

Moreover, this fosters a sense of agency. Your ability to manage your mental health improves when you know your AI partner responds to your needs with personalized strategies. By practicing these micro-interventions, you develop a personalized collection of coping strategies that increase emotional resilience and flexibility.

AI-delivered personalized coping strategies work to develop a resilient mindset that remains adaptable and proactive while staying true to your authentic self. The approach turns emotional regulation into an adaptable process that grows alongside you to help you manage an unpredictable world.

Supplementary Details*

Emotional Trigger Mapping*

The method of emotional trigger mapping involves systematically identifying and recording specific occurrences that generate intense emotional reactions through analysis and documentation. The traditional approach to this method, which requires memory and self-reflection, achieves enhanced capabilities through AI integration because AI can identify recurring patterns within journaling entries as well as physiological and behavioral data. When people learn to identify their emotional triggers clearly, they can replace automatic reactions with deliberate and planned emotional management.

BetterUp Platform*

BetterUp utilizes AI technology to deliver customized coaching services that focus on mental fitness, leadership development, and building emotional resilience. This platform links users to expert coaches while employing artificial intelligence algorithms to monitor emotional patterns and recommend behavioral changes as well as strengthen habits that build resilience. BetterUp combines journaling prompts with mood tracking and interaction analysis to help users achieve emotional clarity and personal growth throughout their journey.

Grit (Angela Duckworth)*

The term grit represents a blend of long-term dedication and unwavering effort to reach goals, as defined by psychologist Angela Duckworth. Grit stands apart from momentary motivation because it requires individuals to endure difficulties while keeping their attention on long-term objectives and continuing to work toward them without immediate gratification. Academic and professional success depends heavily on grit, which serves as an essential predictor and a fundamental component of personal resilience.

Growth Mindset (Carol Dweck)*

The growth mindset stands as psychologist Carol Dweck's concept, which holds that abilities and intelligence can be enhanced through learning and persistent effort. A fixed mindset operates on the principle that characteristics such as intelligence remain constant throughout one's life. When individuals adopt a growth mindset, they learn to see challenges as learning experiences while prioritizing effort above instant success and maintaining their determination through setbacks instead of giving in to defeat.

Predictive Analytics in Mental Health*

Predictive analytics for mental health uses artificial intelligence algorithms to identify future emotional states and psychological requirements in advance of emerging difficulties. AI systems analyze mood logs along with journal entries and biometric data to predict emotional downturns and then suggest proactive coping strategies like breathing exercises and mindfulness practices before individuals feel overwhelmed. Mental health care evolves from a reactionary approach into a preventive framework that anticipates needs before they arise.

Spring Health and Wysa*

• **Spring Health:** Spring Health operates as a complete mental health system that employs machine learning algorithms to develop custom wellness plans for its users. The platform pairs users with therapy and coaching services as well as mindfulness resources while using behavioral analysis and self-reported data to constantly improve its recommendations.

• **Wysa:** A mental health chatbot driven by artificial intelligence called Wysa delivers cognitive behavioral therapy methods along with tools for mood monitoring and strengthening emotional resilience. Wysa acts as a private non-judgmental partner by utilizing conversational AI to help users develop stress reduction and anxiety coping mechanisms along with mood management strategies.

Micro-Coaching Interventions*

Micro-coaching interventions offer real-time personalized coaching prompts aimed at providing immediate support during crucial emotional events. Users get real-time coaching prompts like breathing reminders and confidence-building affirmations through timely nudges based on current emotional data instead of waiting for pre-planned sessions. The designed method delivers coping techniques at critical moments to build emotional resilience through continuous and convenient practice.

Personalized Coping Strategies*
Personalized coping strategies provide adaptive techniques

specifically designed for an individual through analysis of their unique emotional patterns, as well as their lifestyle habits, stress responses, and personal goals. The AI systems develop these strategies by evaluating both the user's historical data and current emotional state to provide personalized interventions such as grounding exercises, breathing practices, or mental reframing techniques that suit the individual best.

Successful Lives Primary Programme: Growth Mindset – Focus Education.
https://www.focus-education.co.uk/products/ successful-lives-primary-programme-growth-mindset

Ch. 8 - Using AI Optimization to Set and Achieve Your Goals

I magine setting a goal not just with hope and determination, but with a precise tool that analyzes your behavior, predicts challenges, and adapts your plan in real time. This is the reality when AI optimization* enters the realm of personal goal setting. No longer must ambition rest solely on willpower; it can be strengthened through intelligent systems that provide structure, feedback, and course corrections throughout the journey.

SMART 2.0 Framework:

• Specific: Goals remain clearly defined but are now refined dynamically based on data.
• Measurable: Progress is consistently quantified and visualized by AI systems.
• Achievable: Objectives adapt by modifying their difficulty level based on real-time performance.
• Relevant: AI personalization helps ensure that goals stay aligned with evolving values and priorities.
• Time-aware: Deadlines become fluid and optimized, balancing urgency with realistic pacing using predictive analytics.

The improved framework recognizes personal goals developed through changing conditions. Your personal growth plans need to adapt because life is constantly changing. AI systems align your goals with current realities to enhance sustainable growth instead of rigid structures. AI optimization requires predictive analytics* because it uses past behavior patterns to make future outcome predictions. Predictive models used in sports and education have transformed how performance training and learning outcomes are developed and delivered.

Elite athletics teams now depend more on AI systems to tailor their training programs. Data from athletes' biometrics combined with sleep patterns and workload metrics enable machine learning models* to forecast injury risks and recommend personalized training adjustments. Coaches who identify rest needs and training adjustments for athletes before issues arise can avoid performance setbacks and extend athletes' career longevity.

Adaptive learning platforms like Carnegie Learning* employ predictive analytics tools to tailor educational curricula to individual student needs. These systems detect student difficulties and supply specific exercises to fill knowledge gaps, which leads to superior understanding rates relative to conventional teaching methods. The applications of these fields demonstrate that predictive systems go beyond problem reaction by forecasting potential issues and delivering timely interventions that keep progress towards objectives on track. The application of this method to personal development converts the pursuit of goals from a strict deadline-oriented race into an adaptable journey that evolves along with life's continuous changes.

Through predictive analytics, individuals can create goals using adaptive strategic planning*. AI tools maintain goal motivation and prevent frustration by dynamically adjusting pathways according to real-world performance rather than setting fixed milestones that become outdated. The ability to adapt transforms challenges into educational experiences that build resilience and lead to lasting achievement.

AI-driven personal goal management can lead to transformative results yet still lacks assurance of success. The analysis of case studies provides insight into the potential benefits and challenges of using AI for goal management while delivering essential guidance for future users (How does generative AI impact creator economies in music? | republica. https://re-publica.com/de/session/how-does-generative-ai-impact-creator-economies-music).

Olivia, who works as a freelance writer, used an AI productivity* platform to structure her everyday tasks along with her writing assignments. The system conducted an analysis of her work patterns to determine when she experienced peak focus and creativity. The system used these insights to optimize her schedule by recommending morning writing sessions followed by afternoon administrative tasks. After three months, Olivia observed her output rise by 40% while also achieving a better work-life balance.

David, an entrepreneur who implemented an advanced AI goal-tracking system, *failed to revise or adjust the AI-generated recommendations. The system developed inefficient work patterns like constant multitasking because it first thought these behaviors indicated productivity. David experienced burnout and frustration since the AI system optimized his work activities without human oversight to guide it towards meaningful* outcomes.

These examples highlight a vital principle: AI delivers powerful tools yet human involvement continues to be indispensable. Successful users engage in an active partnership with their AI systems by critically reviewing suggestions while providing feedback and adjusting parameters when necessary. AI optimization aims to develop self-awareness and better decision-making abilities rather than giving up control.

Personal goal achievement through AI optimization calls for a shift from traditional static goal-setting based on current wishes to dynamic objectives that adjust according to real-world feedback. We need to maintain harmony between our confidence in intelligent systems and our application of human intuition.

Practical steps for maximizing AI-driven goal setting include:
• Regularly review and refine your goals based on AI insights (6 Effective Steps To Create A Successful CRM Strategy For 2024.).
• Consider AI recommendations as starting points, not final commands.
• Prioritize systems that promote transparency and user control over strict automation.
• Embracing flexibility: understanding that adjusting goals signifies intelligence, not failure.
Integrating AI into personal growth results in strengthened resilience and adaptability as well as a closer bond to your changing identity. Through this process you attain your objectives while developing into a more conscious and deliberate individual who transforms technology from a support mechanism to a powerful tool for genuine and enduring change.

Supplemental Details*

AI Optimization*
AI optimization utilizes artificial intelligence algorithms to enhance processes which in this context relates to personal goal setting and achievement. AI systems modify strategies in real-time by studying behavior patterns alongside performance metrics and

environmental data. AI helps people to make informed choices while maintaining their goals and adjusting their objectives without depending only on willpower or manual updates.

SMART 2.0 Framework*

The SMART 2.0 framework updates conventional goal-setting practices through artificial intelligence to create flexible goal components. Goals maintain their Specific nature while being updated through user input as time progresses. Progress becomes Measurable through automated data visualization. Achievable targets are recalibrated based on performance. The system maintains relevance by taking evolving values into account. Time-awareness eliminates fixed deadlines by adopting flexible timing through predictive analytics. SMART 2.0 transforms static goals into adaptable systems that adjust automatically to track personal advancement.

Predictive Analytics*

Predictive analytics uses machine learning and statistical models to analyze current and historical data in order to forecast future outcomes (Bigdata DWBI). Predictive analytics examines behavior patterns along with energy and task performance data to identify possible future challenges and enables preemptive measures in personal development contexts. Proactive insights enable users to adjust their course effectively while preserving their drive and avoiding burnout and stagnation.

Adaptive Strategic Planning*

Adaptive strategic planning functions as a flexible system that uses data to guide people toward their goals. Fixed milestones define traditional planning whereas adaptive strategies dynamically adjust according to real-time user performance metrics along with emotional states and life circumstances. AI systems keep goals realistic by continuously analyzing user input and suggesting necessary changes which maintains user motivation while eliminating disappointment from outdated plans.

Carnegie Learning*

Carnegie Learning provides a personalized learning experience through an adaptive education platform which utilizes artificial intelligence. Through student response tracking and learning gap identification the system delivers real-time lessons that meet specific educational needs. This system demonstrates how predictive AI models can drive educational and personal growth effectively by customizing content for each learner individually.

Machine Learning Models*

Computer algorithms called machine learning models develop their functionality by extracting information from data. These models improve through exposure to large datasets, where they learn patterns rather than following explicitly programmed rules. Machine learning in personal development contexts allows AI systems to comprehend individual habits and preferences for improved predictive accuracy and tailored recommendations.

AI Productivity Platforms / Goal-Tracking Systems*

Digital tools known as AI productivity platforms and goal-tracking systems analyze performance trends by monitoring user activities and provide automated suggestions to enhance time management and focus. Productivity platforms utilize behavior-based metrics including typing velocity, task duration, and break intervals to enhance scheduling and customize task management systems for individual users. The best systems integrate user feedback to make sure their suggestions match human values and objectives.

Human Oversight in AI Systems*

The human-in-the-loop model requires people to stay active decision-makers instead of becoming passive receivers of machine-generated suggestions in AI systems. The approach focuses on intense examination and individualized adjustment coupled with moral scrutiny of AI-generated suggestions. By maintaining control, users can steer systems to produce meaningful results while avoiding overreliance on algorithms that are prone to data misinterpretation.

How does generative AI impact creator economies in music? | Republica. https://re-publica.com/de/session/how-does-generative-ai-impact-creator-economies-music

6 Effective Steps To Create A Successful CRM Strategy For 2024. https://www.leadsquared.com/learn/sales/crm-strategy/

Big Data DWBI. https://www.bigdatadwbi.com/2023/11/

Ch. 9 - Sustaining Growth: Strategies for Reflection, Feedback, and Iterative Learning

G rowth does not follow a straight path because it typically progresses through cycles that include phases of quick advancement followed by stagnant periods where visible progress halts. Understanding this cyclical pattern is essential for maintaining personal development throughout one's lifetime. Real growth demands more than hard work; it demands reflective wisdom to adjust and maintain perseverance despite a lack of immediate results. The process benefits from AI through structured feedback loops* which support ongoing reflection and iterative learning in a manner similar to Agile Methodology.

*Agile Methodology** represents a project management strategy that focuses on iterative advancement through regular feedback and constant improvement instead of fixed long-term planning (Agile Training In Chennai With 100% Placement.). The Agile framework started in software development as a method of adapting to change while prioritizing teamwork above strict planning. The core concepts of iterative development, together with reflection and fast adaptation, extend their usefulness to numerous fields outside the technology sector. Applying Agile principles to personal growth involves creating small achievable objectives while reflecting on results to adjust strategies through feedback and incrementally developing skills rather than anticipating instant expertise.

Software development teams experience personal development through iterative cycles of execution, reflection, and improvement. Personal development aims for steady progress through small improvements instead of attempting to achieve perfection instantly. The Agile team's guiding principle is "fail fast, learn faster." The team conducts evaluations at the end of each sprint work cycle* to discuss successful outcomes and identify improvement areas while planning future strategy adjustments. This methodology converts errors into useful information that guides future successful outcomes. This principle, when applied to personal development, teaches individuals to interpret setbacks as necessary feedback that helps improve future strategies.

Set a personal objective to enhance your ability to manage emotions. You should focus on weekly progress assessments instead of expecting immediate expertise as you reflect upon both your moments of calmness during stressful situations and your challenging episodes. With every review you make modifications to your methods which may include implementing breathing exercises alongside refining journal prompts and adjusting your mindfulness activities.

Leveraging artificial intelligence tools in this continuous cycle speeds up the learning experience. Sentiment analysis* monitors emotional changes through time to detect minor positive shifts and developing difficulties. Personalized prompts steer reflective thinking through questions like "What triggered today's emotional reaction?" or "Which strategies worked best this week?" Reflective insights offer substantial content for development that sustains growth as adaptable and active instead of fixed and unyielding.

Feedback loop systems enable personal development since actions generate responses that direct future actions. In Reinforcement Learning* within machine learning frameworks, an agent improves its decision-making abilities through feedback mechanisms that use rewards and penalties to guide its behavior. The agent gradually adapts its actions throughout time to achieve better results. This principle serves as an effective analogy for understanding human growth.

Your environment provides feedback whenever you practice mindfulness or work towards achieving your goals. Success reinforces beneficial actions, whereas failures provide chances to adjust strategies. Your learning process mirrors how an AI agent improves its strategy through repeated trials, where feedback guides your adaptation instead of perfect performance.

Through structured insights delivered in a timely manner, AI tools improve human feedback loops. A journaling app may demonstrate how practicing gratitude exercises leads to better mood improvements during a two-week period. Productivity tracker results demonstrate that people who work in concentrated sessions achieve greater satisfaction compared to those who multitask. Data-driven insights direct you toward improved strategies that enable you to fine-tune your methods accurately.

Effective use of feedback loops requires adopting a curious mindset instead of making judgments. All feedback received functions merely as informational input regardless of its positive or negative nature. Your value remains unchanged by feedback because it serves only to guide your subsequent actions. The shift turns growth into a dynamic process that becomes engaging rather than a challenging task.

No matter how advanced your feedback system or AI tools might be, plateaus will always occur. Eventually your progress will decelerate and your motivation might diminish while doubts begin to emerge. Understanding that plateaus occur naturally during growth journeys and developing methods to navigate them are key for maintaining long-term development.

When facing a plateau, consider these strategies:
• Revisit your Why: Rediscover the fundamental motivations that drive your objectives. Reassess your initial motivations and the version of yourself you aim to become.
• Shift Focus: Rekindling your drive can occur when you explore additional skills and growth areas that relate to your current path. To rejuvenate your mindfulness practice that feels stagnant try experimenting with mindful movement or creative visualization techniques*.
• Adjust Goals: Leverage AI insights to reassess your objectives. Your initial objective might require transformation as your understanding of yourself develops.
• Celebrate Small Wins: Acknowledge incremental progress. Keeping up with your practice through challenging times deserves celebration as a noteworthy achievement.
• Rest Strategically: When you hit a plateau, it usually signals that your body and mind require rest and a chance to integrate experiences while renewing motivation. Mindful pauses should be seen as essential components that support sustainable growth rather than as setbacks.

Utilizing AI tools during periods of stagnation helps generate new perspectives. The process of trend analysis* combined with past success reflection and the creation of new prompts can disrupt repetitive patterns while delivering fresh motivation for upcoming milestones.

Use plateaus as chances to rest, build strength, reflect on personal growth and ready yourself for upcoming challenges. These experiences prove that you are extending beyond your usual boundaries while developing new abilities and demonstrating strength.

True personal development over time comes from iterative mastery rather than constant advancement. Through understanding that reflection and feedback along with adjustment and patience drive success rather than distract from it.

The combination of artificial intelligence systems with intentional self-reflection and flexible strategies enables you to maintain forward momentum in spite of inevitable obstacles. Growth develops as a resilient dynamic journey which intimately connects with your evolving self.

You create a distinctive path through each cycle of reflection and refinement, which relies on internal wisdom and external intelligent tools for guidance instead of just external metrics.

Supplemental Details*

*Agile Methodology**

Agile methodology was developed as a project management style in software development before expanding to become a universal approach across various industries. This methodology promotes brief planning periods while continuously integrating feedback and iterative development instead of inflexible long-term planning. Agile methodology prioritizes continuous learning over immediate perfection by promoting iterative reflection and experimentation, followed by swift adaptation. Through application to personal development, Agile principles help individuals reach their potential by setting small, attainable objectives and conducting ongoing self-evaluation to progress through repeated testing and improvement.

Sprint Work Cycle*

The sprint work cycle stands as an essential component of Agile Methodology. A sprint work cycle represents a fixed timeframe usually lasting 1–2 weeks dedicated to completing predetermined tasks or objectives. Each sprint concludes with a review where individuals or teams analyze their results to understand successes and failures and apply these insights toward future improvements. This technique boosts flexibility and forward movement by dividing big objectives into achievable segments with integrated milestones.

Structured Feedback Loops*

The structured feedback loop functions as an ongoing cycle where actions lead to observations of outcomes, while responses such as results, emotions, or data analysis guide subsequent behavior. Feedback loops help people make changes based on successful actions while eliminating ineffective behaviors, which parallels how AI systems learn and improve through performance analysis over time. The reflective cycle maintains continuous growth by keeping it responsive and sustainable.

Sentiment Analysis*

Sentiment analysis works as an artificial intelligence method for decoding emotional meaning from textual and spoken communication. AI systems determine emotional tone in journal entries or messages through analysis of word choice and phrasing patterns. The analytical process reveals emotional patterns and trends that remain hidden from individuals and sheds light on mood development and the underlying causes of emotional peaks and valleys.

Reinforcement Learning (AI Context)*

In reinforcement learning, an AI agent optimizes its actions through a trial-and-error process that involves receiving rewards for successful behaviors while getting penalized for mistakes. As time passes, the agent enhances its decision-making abilities while improving its results. This methodology replicates human development since failures provide learning opportunities while persistent effort produces improved results. When we apply this model to personal advancement, we see that feedback plays a fundamental role in achieving mastery rather than perfection.

AI-Enhanced Journaling / Productivity Trackers*

Digital platforms that function as AI-enhanced journaling tools and productivity trackers gather personal data, including mood entries and task completion patterns, to create individualized feedback through analysis. Sentiment analysis combined with pattern recognition and trend monitoring helps users identify the elements that influence their performance and well-being through these analytical tools. Their visual insights, along with adaptive recommendations, help people establish clearer goals while managing their emotions effectively.

Trend Analysis*

The process of trend analysis involves the detection of data patterns and shifts throughout time. AI systems apply trend analysis to personal development by tracking changes in performance levels as well as emotional and behavioral progress. These insights allow individuals to recognize progress stages while identifying areas of stagnation and potential adjustments for momentum restoration.

Mindful Movement / Creative Visualization*

• Mindful Movement:

Mindful movement merges physical activities with intentional awareness to transform daily activities like walking and light yoga into meditative practices. Directing attention to the body strengthens presence while simultaneously helping to relieve emotional strain.

• Creative Visualization:

Creative visualization requires guided imagery to practice mental success rehearsals and visualize peaceful states or anticipated achievements. The technique activates brain motivational circuits while building confidence through a detailed mental focus on intended results.

Agile Training in Chennai with 100% Placement. https://www.softlogicsys.in/agile-training-in-chennai/

Ch. 10 - Conclusion: AI and the Future of Personal Growth

W hen you arrive at your journey's conclusion, take a moment to pause and reflect.

Your journey has taken you through a realm where artificial intelligence stands as more than a technological wonder but transforms into a guiding partner that illuminates and augments the most profound areas of personal growth.

Our journey has shown that AI extends beyond simple code and data-processing algorithms. Careful integration transforms artificial intelligence into a reflective surface alongside a mentor and an enabling force.

Sentiment analysis* enables us to gain insight into our emotional patterns.
The prediction of stress triggers helps us cultivate mindfulness.
Through personalized micro-coaching* our resilience grows,
which enhances our recovery abilities after experiencing setbacks.
The system transforms achievement into a dynamic and evolving
pursuit while optimizing our objectives instead of presenting a
fixed endpoint.
Our growth remains continuous as we incorporate reflection and iterative learning into our everyday routines. Personal development in the future will involve conscious collaborations with intelligent systems instead of relinquishing control to machines.

The beginning of a new age unites emotional intelligence and artificial intelligence in a mutually reinforcing relationship. Future success will depend not just on effort and discipline but also require adaptability along with insight and openness to intelligent feedback. By 2030, AI technology will combine with personal development to create unparalleled levels of integration.

We can expect:

A coaching experience that personalizes itself to each life phase while helping us navigate career changes and relationship dynamics and personal ambition development.

AI companions capable of understanding emotions* provide detailed support which enhances self-awareness without substituting human interactions.

Transparent AI tools *within ethical self-optimization ecosystems* enable people to maintain privacy protection while pursuing growth opportunities.

Predictive resilience frameworks* help systems anticipate challenges ahead of time so we can prepare and improve our ability to adapt to an ever-changing world (adaptogens adaptogenic herbs dr. nikolai lazaret romeo mori).

Yet, with this power comes responsibility. Every person needs to maintain constant vigilance to protect their independence. Continual reflection is essential to maintain ethical standards when using AI to advance personal development. Do we choose tools that protect our privacy and uphold our dignity? Are our AI applications driving true personal advancement rather than chasing empty performance indicators?

How well do we maintain a balance between efficiency and

humanity while aligning productivity with well-being? The new era requires individuals to master lifelong adaptability* as their defining capability. Technologies will evolve, and tools will change. Personal growth relies on our timeless pursuit to comprehend ourselves while broadening our abilities and living with purpose. Significant transformations occur when we combine the accuracy of artificial intelligence with self-awareness insights. Technology becomes a guiding light that illuminates paths previously hidden to us when we operate it not as a support but as a lantern. Growth requires daily practice through humble courage and hopeful effort instead of being a one-time achievement.

You now possess a new set of tools and a new lens through which to view your journey. The next step belongs to you. Choose intentionally. Reflect often. Adapt courageously.

And remember: the most extraordinary version of yourself is not something artificial intelligence will create for you. It is the version you will craft thoughtfully, authentically, and resiliently, with AI as a trusted companion on the path.

The future is not something we await passively. It is something we actively create with every choice, every insight, and every step forward. May your journey be wise, empowered, and filled with transformative growth.

Supplemental Details*

Sentiment Analysis*

Sentiment analysis utilizes artificial intelligence to examine written or spoken language and identify whether the expressed emotions are positive, negative, or neutral. Sentiment analysis reveals emotional patterns over time which enables users to understand their emotional well-being better and stimulates informed introspection and personal development.

Personalized Micro-Coaching*

AI systems provide brief real-time guidance through personalized micro-coaching during essential moments when users need it most. These interventions are customized based on the user's behavior patterns and emotional state to deliver encouragement and coping strategies at optimal times. Micro-coaching builds resilience by providing users with consistent support as they face daily obstacles.

Predictive Resilience Frameworks*

AI-driven predictive resilience frameworks utilize historical and real-time personal data to identify potential emotional obstacles and stress triggers before they happen. The systems offer proactive recommendations for coping methods and mindfulness training while adjusting goals to help people build emotional resilience and flexibility before facing unknown future situations.

Transparent AI Tools*

The design of transparent AI tools includes processes that make decision-making and prediction logic understandable to users. These systems reveal their internal decision-making processes so users can understand and assess AI logic, which builds trust and supports ethical awareness and better decision-making.

Ethical Self-Optimization Ecosystems*

Ethical self-optimization ecosystems act as integrated personal development platforms that focus on performance advancement while maintaining strong principles around human dignity, privacy protection, and individual autonomy. Users of these ecosystems can achieve personal development while keeping their data secure and ensuring their technology usage aligns with their values and ethical beliefs.

AI Companions Capable of Understanding Emotions*

These sophisticated AI companions that understand emotions can detect user feelings and respond with empathetic engagement. AI systems provide compassionate interactions to support emotional well-being instead of basic task execution like functional tools. These systems function as supportive aids alongside human relationships without replacing them while helping users build resilience through self-reflection.

Mastering Lifelong Adaptability*

To achieve lifelong adaptability requires people to continuously develop their ability to modify mindsets while learning new approaches and altering behaviors based on technological changes as well as shifts in life stages and personal objectives. Adaptability guarantees that growth continues to be achievable and meaningful while maintaining strength through external changes in the fast-paced world.

adaptogens adaptogenic herbs dr. nikolai lazaret romeo mori. https://humanshiftpaper.com/stories/adaptogens-adatogenic-herbs/

Thank You

 Final Note from the Author.

Thank you for taking the time to read this book. I truly hope the insights and strategies shared within these pages have been both informative and empowering for your journey.

If you found this book valuable, I would deeply appreciate it if you could leave a brief review. Your feedback not only helps others discover this resource, but it also supports the continued development of future content that serves readers like you.

You can leave your review here:

{Page Link}

With sincere gratitude,
John Workman, Ph.D.

Appendix A: Key Terms & Definitions

1. Artificial Intelligence (AI)
   A branch of computer science focused on building systems that can perform tasks typically requiring human intelligence, such as learning, decision-making, and pattern recognition.

   ,

2. Machine Learning (ML)
   A subset of AI where computers learn from data to make predictions or decisions without being explicitly programmed for every task.

3. Algorithm
   A step-by-step set of instructions or rules a computer follows to solve a problem or complete a task.

4. Neural Network
   A computer system modeled after the human brain's network of neurons. It processes information by recognizing patterns in large amounts of data and is often used in image and speech recognition.

5. Deep Learning
   An advanced type of machine learning that uses multi-layered neural networks to analyze complex patterns. It powers technologies like voice assistants and recommendation systems.

6. Natural Language Processing (NLP)
   A field of AI that helps machines understand, interpret, and generate human language. It's what allows AI tools to

understand your voice commands or chat with you through text.

7. Chatbot
A software application that uses NLP to simulate conversation with users, often found in customer service, websites, and personal development tools.

'

8. Personalization Engine
An AI system that tailors content, suggestions, or experiences based on a user's data, preferences, and behavior, commonly used in apps like fitness trackers or digital learning platforms.

9. Predictive Analytics
The practice of using historical data and machine learning to forecast future trends or behaviors—useful in habit tracking, productivity analysis, and goal planning.

10. Data Bias
When AI systems produce unfair or unbalanced results due to imbalanced or non-representative training data, which can reflect human or systemic biases.

11. Feedback Loop (in AI)
A cyclical process where an AI system uses its previous outputs and user interactions as new inputs, learning and refining its responses over time.

'

12. Digital Twin (Self)
A digital representation of a person's behavior, goals, or habits, often created using AI to simulate and optimize personal development strategies.

13. Human-in-the-Loop (HITL)
An AI development approach that keeps humans actively

involved in the decision-making or training process to improve accuracy and accountability.

14. Prompt Engineering
The craft of designing effective inputs (questions or commands) to get desired outputs from AI systems, especially in natural language interfaces.

15. Cognitive Augmentation
Using AI to enhance human thinking, memory, or learning, supporting decision-making, creativity, and self-reflection.

16. Artificial General Intelligence (AGI)
A hypothetical form of AI capable of performing any intellectual task a human can do. Unlike today's narrow AI, AGI would possess flexible reasoning and adaptive learning across all domains.

17. Consciousness (Machine vs. Human)
In AI discussions, consciousness refers to self-awareness or subjective experience. Though machines currently do not possess consciousness, the concept raises questions about identity, morality, and the limits of simulation.

18. Algorithmic Selfhood
A conceptual term describing how individuals may construct aspects of their identity through feedback from algorithm-driven platforms — e.g., how recommendation systems reinforce personal beliefs, habits, or aesthetics.

19. Quantified Self
A movement that uses technology to collect data on personal habits, behaviors, and biological functions, turning introspection into a form of data-driven analysis.

The integration of digital or AI tools into practices of mindfulness, purpose, and transcendence suggests that technology can support spiritual growth rather than replace it.

20. Techno-Spirituality
    The integration of digital or AI tools into practices of mindfulness, purpose, and transcendence — suggesting that technology can support spiritual growth rather than replace it.

21. Ethical AI
    A framework for designing and applying AI systems in ways that respect human dignity, fairness, privacy, and transparency is particularly important when using AI to influence behavior or personal decision-making.
    An individual's capacity to consciously shape their digital presence, data interactions, and technology use, as opposed to passively being shaped by algorithms.

22. Digital Agency
    An individual's capacity to consciously shape their digital presence, data interactions, and technology use — opposed to passively being shaped by algorithms.

23. Behavioral Nudging (via AI)
    The use of AI to subtly guide user decisions — through interface design, reminders, or feedback — raises ethical considerations about autonomy and influence in personal development tools.

24. Existential Risk (AI-Related)
    Concerns related to scenarios where AI development could result in irreversible harm to humanity. While more relevant to AGI, it's worth reflecting on how such possibilities influence personal tech ethics.

25. Human-Centered AI
    Designing AI systems to augment human values, capabilities,

and well-being is central to the thesis that AI should empower rather than replace human agency in the transformation journey.

26. Digital Minimalism
A philosophy advocating intentional technology use, especially relevant in AI contexts, so that tools serve well-being and growth rather than distraction or dependency.
by algorithmic suggestions and prompts

27. Algorithmic Determinism
The notion that personal choices may be increasingly influenced — or even pre-determined — by algorithmic suggestions prompts reflection on free will and self-directed growth.

28. Reflective Loop (Human-AI Symbiosis)
An ongoing, conscious interaction between human intention and machine feedback. In personal transformation, this loop fosters a deeper awareness of one's behavioral data and developmental trajectory.
enhances efficiency, but

29. Cognitive Offloading
The process of outsourcing thinking tasks (e.g., reminders, analysis, decision-making) to AI tools enhances efficiency, but it raises questions about dependence and loss of internal cognitive strength.

30. Digital Mindfulness
A practice that encourages conscious awareness of how we interact with digital tools, including AI, aiming to use them as aids for focus, clarity, and presence rather than distractions.

Appendix B: AI Tools & Platforms for Personal Use

T his appendix introduces you to a curated selection of AI-powered tools and platforms that support various aspects of personal development. Each entry includes the tool's primary function, intended personal application, and potential benefits. All tools listed are either free or offer accessible entry points for individual users (as of 2025).

1. ChatGPT (OpenAI)
- Function: Conversational AI and personal assistant
- Use Case: Journaling, self-coaching, goal clarification, decision support
- Benefit: Offers real-time reflective dialogue, idea generation, emotional processing, and educational support.
- Website: https://chat.openai.com

2. Notion AI
- Function: Productivity and note-taking enhanced by AI
- Use Case: Organizing personal knowledge, tracking habits, and summarizing tasks
- Benefit: Helps manage routines, extract insights from journals, and streamline goal planning.
- Website: https://www.notion.so

3. Replika
- Function: AI-powered emotional companion

- Use Case: Daily check-ins, stress relief, guided self-dialogue
- Benefit: Offers a safe environment for emotional exploration and mental clarity.
- Website: https://replika.com

4. Youper
- Function: AI-based mental health assistant
- Use Case: Mood tracking, cognitive-behavioral therapy (CBT) exercises
- Benefit: Supports emotional regulation and mental fitness through evidence-based approaches.
- Website: https://www.youper.ai

5. Otter.ai
- Function: AI-powered transcription and summarization
- Use Case: Recording and reviewing self-reflection sessions or voice journals
- Benefit: Converts spoken thoughts into searchable, structured text — ideal for reflective analysis.
- Website: https://otter.ai

6. Grammarly (with AI Writing Assistant)
- Function: Writing enhancement tool with contextual feedback
- Use Case: Journaling, email clarity, thought structuring
- Benefit: Helps refine expression and tone, useful for clear goal articulation or self-communication.
- Website: https://www.grammarly.com

7. Mindsera
- Function: AI-powered journaling and mindset coaching
- Use Case: Structured journaling, resilience building, daily insights

- Benefit: Provides cognitive-behavioral prompts and generates personalized reflections.
- Website: https://www.mindsera.com

8. Feedly (with Leo AI)
- Function: Personalized content aggregation and summarization
- Use Case: Lifelong learning, staying informed on topics like productivity and well-being
- Benefit: Helps filter information overload and align content consumption with personal goals.
- Website: https://feedly.com

9. Descript (with AI Editing Tools)
- Function: Multimedia editing and transcription
- Use Case: Self-recording reviews, creating personal development vlogs or podcasts
- Benefit: Allows reflective practice through audiovisual media and editing-based self-insight.
- Website: https://www.descript.com

10. Focusmate
- Function: AI-assisted virtual co-working
- Use Case: Overcoming procrastination, accountability
- Benefit: Supports productivity by creating structured focus sessions with gentle AI reminders.
- Website: https://www.focusmate.com

11. Earkick
- Function: AI-based mental health tracker
- Use Case: Tracking stress, anxiety, and mental health patterns
- Benefit: Uses short daily inputs to detect trends and provide data-driven well-being insights.

- Website: https://www.earkick.com

12. Reflectly
- Function: AI-guided journal for gratitude and positivity
- Use Case: Building optimism and emotional awareness
- Benefit: Promotes emotional growth with gentle prompts and motivational insights.
- Website: https://www.reflectly.app

Note to Readers:

The inclusion of these platforms does not imply endorsement of any single tool, nor does this list represent an exhaustive inventory. Readers are encouraged to experiment with what aligns best with their personal goals and values, and to remain mindful of data privacy policies when using AI-powered tools.

Appendix C: Practical Exercises & Reflections

T his appendix provides you with actionable exercises designed to reinforce the book's key ideas. Each activity integrates AI tools or AI-informed methods and is accompanied by a reflective prompt to encourage deeper personal insight. These exercises are intended to be flexible and repeatable across various stages of a reader's transformation journey.

1. AI-Assisted Vision Statement Generator

Objective: Clarify your personal development goals using an AI writing assistant (e.g., ChatGPT or Notion AI).

• Instructions:

1. Prompt your AI assistant: "Help me draft a personal vision statement that reflects my core values, long-term goals, and strengths."

2. Iterate on the draft, adding specificity and emotional resonance.
   • Reflection Prompt:
   Which parts of the AI-generated response felt aligned with your inner truth? Which parts felt artificial or misaligned—and why?

2. Pattern Recognition Through Journaling

Objective: Identify recurring thoughts, behaviors, and emotional patterns using AI-supported journaling (e.g., Mindsera or Reflectly).

• Instructions:

3. Commit to journaling daily for 7 days.

4. Use AI analysis tools (or manually tag entries) to identify trends in language use, emotional tone, and themes.
   • Reflection Prompt:
   What patterns emerged that surprised you? How do these patterns inform your next steps in personal transformation?

3. Digital Mirror Exercise: "Ask the AI About Me"
Objective: Use conversational AI as a reflective tool to uncover blind spots or affirm strengths.

• Instructions:

5. Ask: "Based on how I describe my life, what strengths and values do you see in me?"

6. Continue with: "What limiting beliefs might I be holding on to, based on our conversation?"
   • Reflection Prompt:
   Did the AI's interpretation offer new insights or merely reflect your current self-view?

4. AI-Enhanced Habit Formation Tracker
Objective: Set up and analyze a habit using AI-driven platforms (e.g., Notion AI, Youper, or a spreadsheet with GPT assistance).

• Instructions:

7. Choose one habit you want to build (e.g., morning stretching).

8. Track behavior for 14 days.

9. Use AI to analyze: "What does this data say about my consistency and triggers?"
   • Reflection Prompt:
   What internal or environmental factors contributed to your

success or struggle?

5. Values Clarification Through Semantic AI
Objective: Use an AI assistant to explore your personal values through definition, contrast, and prioritization.

• Instructions:

10. Ask the AI: "List 30 common personal values. Help me narrow them to the five that define my life purpose."

11. Engage in a back-and-forth discussion about each selected value's importance and practical expression.
    • Reflection Prompt:
    Which values feel authentically yours, and which feel socially imposed or aspirational?

6. Time Audit with AI Categorization
Objective: Assess how your time aligns with your priorities using AI to classify activities.

• Instructions:

12. Log your daily activities for 3–5 days.

13. Ask the AI to group them into categories (e.g., productive, restorative, passive, distracted).

14. Analyze the balance.
    Reflection Prompt:
    What discrepancies do you notice between your stated priorities and your time investment?

7. AI-Driven Decision Matrix
Objective: Improve decision-making by using AI to simulate outcomes and weight criteria.

• Instructions:

15. Define a significant decision.

16. Ask the AI: "Help me build a decision matrix weighing my options by outcome, risk, value alignment, and emotional cost."
    • Reflection Prompt:
    How did adding structure to the decision process affect your emotional response to uncertainty?

8. Resilience Simulation with Hypothetical Scenarios
Objective: Build adaptive thinking using hypothetical challenges generated by AI.
• Instructions:

17. Ask: "Simulate a professional or personal setback. How might I respond to regain momentum?"

18. Use AI feedback to prepare coping strategies.
    • Reflection Prompt:
    What did the simulated response reveal about your current level of resilience and adaptability?

9. Future Self Dialogue
Objective: Envision your future self and engage in dialogue using AI as an imaginative tool.
• Instructions:

19. Ask AI: "Act as my future self, 10 years from now, successful and fulfilled. What advice do you have for me today?"

20. Record and reflect on the conversation.
    • Reflection Prompt:
    What emotions arose during this interaction? Did your future self say what you needed to hear, or what you feared?

10. Digital Detox Assessment

Objective: Use AI to evaluate your relationship with digital tools and social media.

• Instructions:

21. Ask AI to conduct a self-assessment quiz: "Evaluate my screen time habits, attention focus, and content consumption patterns."

22. Identify what tools or platforms are helping vs. hindering growth.

• Reflection Prompt:

What changes could you make to realign your digital environment with your values and mental clarity?

Appendix D: Sample AI-Powered Routines or Journals

T his appendix offers structured, real-world examples of how to integrate AI into daily routines and journaling practices for sustained personal growth. Each sample is designed to demonstrate the practical implementation of AI tools discussed in the book, emphasizing reflection, consistency, and data-informed insights.

1. Morning Clarity Routine (Using Notion AI or ChatGPT)
Purpose: Center your focus, clarify intentions, and align your day with long-term goals.
Sample Routine:
Time: 10–15 minutes (first thing in the morning)

1. Prompt AI: "Help me define my top three priorities for today based on my goals from this week."

2. Mindset Check: "Describe how I feel this morning and what thoughts are dominating my attention."

3. Intention Setting: "Generate a short affirmation that reflects my values and today's objectives."
   Example Journal Output:
   • Top 3 Priorities: Complete proposal draft, 30-minute workout, reconnect with a mentor
   • Mood Description: Energized but mildly anxious
   • Affirmation: "I lead with clarity and energy, even when outcomes are uncertain."

2. Evening Reflection Routine (Using Reflectly or Mindsera)

Purpose: Promote emotional processing, celebrate progress, and close the day with intentionality.
Sample Routine:
Time: 10 minutes (before bed)

4. Mood Input: Log emotional state on a scale or in free-text

5. AI Prompt: "Summarize my emotional and behavioral patterns for today."

6. Growth Inquiry: "What lesson did I learn today, and how will it shape tomorrow?"
Example Journal Output:
• Mood: Calm, reflective
• Pattern: High focus in the morning, drop in motivation after lunch
• Lesson: Taking a mindful pause helped restore focus — plan a mid-afternoon reset break tomorrow

3. Weekly Review Session (Using Notion AI + ChatGPT)

Purpose: Audit your actions and mindset over the past week and adjust strategies.
Sample Routine:
Time: 30–45 minutes (end of week)

7. Data Review: Export data from habit trackers, journals, or productivity logs

8. Prompt AI: "Analyze my entries and suggest themes, wins, and areas needing attention."

9. Reflection Questions:
o What am I proud of this week?
o What challenged me, and how did I respond?
o What one behavior would make the biggest impact next week?

Example Output:

• Wins: Completed 4 workouts, avoided reactive email checking

• Challenges: Sleep inconsistency

• Next Focus: Reinforce a pre-bed digital wind-down routine

4. Emotional Awareness Micro-Journal (Using Youper or ChatGPT)

Purpose: Increase emotional intelligence through rapid, AI-guided reflection.

Sample Routine:

Time: 3–5 minutes (during stress or after a triggering event)

10. Trigger Entry: Describe what happened

11. AI Prompt: "What emotion am I likely experiencing? What cognitive distortions may be present?"

12. Cognitive Reframe: Ask: "Offer a grounded alternative interpretation of this situation."

    Example Entry:

    • Event: Criticism from a colleague during a meeting

    • AI Analysis: Emotion: Embarrassment → Cognitive distortion: Catastrophizing

    • Reframe: "A moment of critique is not a total failure. It's feedback, not a judgment."

    a

5. Goal Alignment Monthly Check-In (Using ChatGPT or Mindsera)

Purpose: Reassess long-term goals and ensure current actions are still aligned.

Sample Routine:

Time: 30 minutes (monthly)

13. Prompt AI: "List the goals I've been working on this month. Have my actions aligned with them?"

14. Visualization: "Describe the version of me who has fully embodied these goals."

15. Next Steps: "What 3 strategic shifts would better align me with my vision?"
Example Journal Output:
- Misalignment: Too much reactive work, little time on learning goals
- Future Self: Lifelong learner with structured thinking and calm decisiveness
- Strategic Shifts: Block time for reading, delegate admin tasks, schedule reflection breaks

6. Creativity Catalyst Session (Using AI Idea Generators)
Purpose: Unlock creative potential and problem-solving using generative AI.
Sample Routine:
Time: 20 minutes (as needed)

16. Prompt AI: "Brainstorm 10 ways I can creatively solve [insert challenge]."

17. Rank & Evaluate: Rate each idea for feasibility and inspiration

18. Action Prompt: "Turn one idea into a 3-step action plan."
Example Challenge: Feeling disconnected from work
AI Output:
- Top Idea: Start a "behind-the-scenes" podcast about my work process
- 3-Step Plan: Draft episode outline → Record pilot → Share with peers

7. AI-Generated Mindfulness Practice
Purpose: Use AI to generate custom mindfulness or meditation sessions based on current needs.

Sample Routine:

Time: 10 minutes (anytime grounding is needed)

19. Prompt AI: "Create a 5-minute guided meditation script focused on letting go of anxiety."

20. Read or record the script for use

21. Post-session Prompt: "What is one insight or sensation that stayed with me?"
Example Insight: "I noticed how tight my chest was, and how slow breathing softened it."

Appendix E: Curated Resources & Recommended Reading

T his appendix presents a selection of books, articles, academic research, and online resources that expand upon the themes of AI, personal development, digital ethics, and human potential. These recommendations are curated to support further exploration, critical thinking, and practical application beyond the core content of this book.

Books on AI and Society

1. "Life 3.0: Being Human in the Age of Artificial Intelligence" – Max Tegmark
   o explores the long-term implications of AI on society, ethics, and human identity.
   o Recommended for: Readers interested in philosophical and future-oriented AI discussions.

2. "AI 2041: Ten Visions for Our Future" – Kai-Fu Lee & Chen Qiufan
   o Combines fiction and nonfiction to present practical and ethical questions surrounding AI over the next two decades.

3. "Human Compatible: Artificial Intelligence and the Problem of Control" – Stuart Russell
   o A foundational work on aligning AI systems with human values and safety.

Books on Personal Development and Digital Behavior

4. "Atomic Habits" – James Clear
   o Offers a framework for habit formation grounded in identity and behavior design — aligns well with AI-assisted self-tracking.

5. "Deep Work" – Cal Newport
   o Advocates for focused, high-quality productivity in an age of digital distraction.

6. "Digital Minimalism" – Cal Newport
   o A practical guide to intentional technology use — essential for readers exploring AI with balance and discipline.

   Books Bridging Psychology, Technology, and Ethics

7. "The Age of Surveillance Capitalism" – Shoshana Zuboff
   o Critiques how data-driven platforms shape behavior and decision-making in ways that can undermine autonomy.

8. "Reclaiming Conversation: The Power of Talk in a Digital Age" – Sherry Turkle
   o Examines how technology reshapes human interaction, attention, and self-awareness.

9. "Tools of Titans" – Tim Ferriss
   A compendium of habits and strategies from high performers, including those using AI tools for self-optimization.
   A compendium
   Academic Journals and Research Sources

10. Journal of Artificial Intelligence Research (JAIR)
    • Peer-reviewed research articles on machine learning, NLP, and AI ethics.

11. Nature: Machine Intelligence
    • High-quality, multidisciplinary research on AI and its broader implications.

12. AI & Society (Springer)
    • A critical journal addressing cultural, ethical, and societal dimensions of AI.

Online Courses & Learning Platforms

13. Elements of AI (University of Helsinki + Reaktor)
    • A free, beginner-friendly course designed to introduce the basics of AI and its social context.
    • Website: https://www.elementsofai.com

14. Coursera – "AI for Everyone" (Andrew Ng)
    • A widely praised course that explains how AI affects work and personal life from a non-technical perspective.

15. edX – Ethics of AI and Big Data (Linux Foundation)
    • A course exploring data rights, algorithmic fairness, and ethical design.

Selected Articles and Thought Leadership

16. "The AI Mirror: What Machines Teach Us About Ourselves" – MIT Technology Review
    • Reflects on how AI reveals human assumptions, desires, and cognitive biases.

17. "AI and the Future of Mindfulness" – Harvard Business Review

    • Investigates how AI can enhance self-awareness and emotional regulation.

18. "Algorithmic Self-Determination" – IEEE Spectrum
    • Discusses personal data sovereignty and designing AI that respects individual agency.

Organizations and Think Tanks to Follow

19. The Center for Humane Technology
    • Advocates for ethical tech development and digital wellness.
    • Website: https://www.humanetech.com

20. The Future of Life Institute
    • Focuses on existential risk and long-term AI safety.
    • Website: https://futureoflife.org

21. AI Now Institute (NYU)
    • Researches social implications of AI, including labor, rights, and justice.
    • Website: https://ainowinstitute.org

Note to Readers

Resources are selected for their educational value and thought-provoking perspectives. As the AI landscape rapidly evolves, readers are encouraged to seek updated sources, maintain a reflective approach, and critically evaluate the tools and narratives that shape their personal development.

Appendix F: Common Myths & Misconceptions

T his appendix addresses widespread misunderstandings about artificial intelligence, particularly as they relate to personal use, self-development, and digital behavior. Each entry clarifies the myth, explains its origin, and offers a fact-based correction to guide informed engagement with AI tools.

1. Myth: "AI will replace human intuition and creativity."
• Reality: AI complements — but does not replicate — human intuition. While AI can simulate creativity (e.g., generating music or text), it lacks lived experience and emotional context. Personal transformation requires reflective judgment and emotional insight that AI can enhance, but not replace.

2. Myth: "Using AI tools makes self-development artificial or less authentic."
• Reality: Tools are only as artificial as the intent behind their use. When guided by self-awareness and ethical practice, AI can serve as a mirror and catalyst for authentic growth, not a barrier to it.

3. Myth: "AI knows everything and gives objectively correct advice."
• Reality: AI models are trained on historical data and probabilistic reasoning. They do not "understand" in a human sense and may reflect biases, errors, or incomplete information. Human discernment is essential when interpreting AI-generated suggestions.

4. Myth: "You have to be a tech expert to use AI in your daily life."
• Reality: Many AI tools are now designed with user-friendly interfaces and guided prompts. From journaling assistants to decision-making aids, most modern AI applications require no coding or technical background.

5. Myth: "AI applications are too impersonal for emotional or psychological growth."
• Reality: While AI lacks emotion, it can facilitate emotional growth by offering structured prompts, mood analysis, and cognitive-behavioral feedback. Its neutrality can create a safe space for reflection, especially when human support is unavailable.

6. Myth: "AI tools collect your thoughts and use them against you."
• Reality: Privacy concerns are valid, but not all AI tools exploit data. Many platforms allow local storage or anonymized use. Responsible selection of tools, with transparent privacy policies, is critical for secure engagement.
Responsible selection of tools, with transparent privacy policies, is critical for secure engagement.

7. Myth: "AI only benefits high-performance individuals or tech professionals."
• Reality: AI's benefits extend to anyone interested in growth, whether managing anxiety, building routines, or exploring new ideas. Its accessibility makes it valuable across educational, professional, and wellness contexts.

8. Myth: "Once I start using AI, I might lose my ability to think independently."

• Reality: AI should be viewed as a thinking partner, not a replacement. With proper boundaries, it can sharpen critical thinking by offering alternative perspectives or modeling structured problem-solving.

9. Myth: "All AI is the same."
• Reality: AI varies widely—some tools specialize in language, others in pattern recognition, visual generation, or data analytics. Their underlying models, capabilities, and purposes differ significantly.

10. Myth: "AI is neutral and cannot be biased."
• Reality: AI systems reflect the data they are trained on, and that data often carries historical, cultural, or systemic biases. Awareness of bias is essential when using AI for reflection, planning, or personal insight.

11. Myth: "AI can fully understand who I am."
• Reality: AI can analyze patterns and offer insights, but it cannot understand your inner world, values, or lived experience with human depth. Personal identity and transformation remain deeply human processes.

12. Myth: "Using AI to make decisions is lazy or irresponsible."
• Reality: Delegating certain decisions to AI, when done intentionally, can free cognitive energy for higher-order thinking. Responsible users define what to outsource and what to keep under personal deliberation.
• Reality: Delegating certain decisions to AI, when done intentionally, can free cognitive energy for higher-order thinking.

Closing Note:

Awareness of these myths enables more mindful and empowering engagement with AI. The key is not to reject or idolize technology, but to approach it as a tool that, when used consciously, can amplify your journey toward clarity, purpose, and growth.

Glossary

This glossary provides concise, reader-friendly definitions of key terms used throughout the book. It serves as a quick reference for understanding both technical and conceptual language in the context of AI-driven personal development.

A
• Algorithm: A set of instructions or rules followed by a computer to solve a problem or complete a task.
• Artificial Intelligence (AI): The capability of machines to perform tasks that typically require human intelligence, such as learning, decision-making, and pattern recognition.
• Artificial General Intelligence (AGI): A theoretical form of AI with the ability to understand, learn, and apply knowledge across any domain, similar to human intelligence.
• Augmented Intelligence: The use of AI to enhance—not replace—human decision-making and cognition.

B
• Bias (Algorithmic): Systematic errors in AI outcomes caused by flawed or unrepresentative training data, often reflecting human or cultural prejudices.
• Behavioral Nudging: The use of subtle prompts or design elements, often AI-generated, to influence decision-making or behavior.

C
• Chatbot: An AI-driven software application designed to simulate

conversation with users, often through text or voice.

• Cognitive Augmentation: Enhancing human mental functions like memory, focus, or learning using AI tools.

• Consciousness (in AI): A debated concept referring to whether AI can or should possess awareness, emotion, or subjective experience (AI currently does not).

D

• Data-Driven Decision Making: The process of making choices based on analysis and interpretation of data, often supported by AI.

• Deep Learning: A form of machine learning using layered neural networks to recognize complex patterns in data.

• Digital Agency: The capacity of individuals to intentionally control and shape their digital interactions and data presence.

• Digital Minimalism: A lifestyle approach advocating intentional and limited technology use to enhance focus and well-being.

E

• Ethical AI: The practice of designing and applying AI systems in ways that respect human values, dignity, and fairness.

• Existential Risk (AI-related): The potential for advanced AI to pose large-scale threats to humanity's future if not carefully aligned with human interests.

F

• Feedback Loop (AI): A system in which outputs are fed back as inputs for learning and refinement—used by AI to improve performance over time.

H

• Human-Centered AI: Designing AI systems to support, empower,

and align with human values and capacities.
• Human-in-the-Loop (HITL): A design framework where humans remain actively involved in AI systems to guide, supervise, or correct outcomes.

J
• Journaling (AI-powered): Using AI tools to support reflective writing, pattern recognition, and emotional tracking in personal development.

M
• Machine Learning (ML): A subset of AI where systems learn from data to make predictions or decisions without explicit programming.
• Mindfulness (Digital/AI-supported): The practice of being present and aware, enhanced through technology-guided meditation, breathing, or reflection tools.

N
• Natural Language Processing (NLP): A field of AI focused on enabling machines to understand, interpret, and generate human language.
• Neural Network: A computing system modeled after the human brain that processes data through interconnected nodes or "neurons."

P
• Personalization Engine: An AI system that tailors content or experiences based on a user's data and behavior.
• Predictive Analytics: Using data and AI to forecast future trends, behaviors, or outcomes.
• Prompt Engineering: The practice of crafting effective inputs

(questions or instructions) to elicit specific outputs from AI models.

Q
• Quantified Self: The use of digital tools and data collection to track personal behaviors, habits, and physiological patterns.

R
• Reflective Loop (Human-AI Interaction): An intentional cycle of thought and feedback involving AI tools and self-awareness practices.

S
• Selfhood (Algorithmic): The evolving concept of identity is shaped or influenced by algorithmic outputs and feedback mechanisms.
• Surveillance Capitalism: A term describing how companies commodify personal data through surveillance and algorithmic prediction for profit.

T
• Techno-Spirituality: The use of technology, especially AI, to deepen practices of mindfulness, purpose, and spiritual self-exploration.

V
• Values Alignment (in AI): Ensuring that AI tools reflect and reinforce the user's core values rather than contradicting or manipulating them.
• Vision Statement (AI-assisted): A concise expression of a person's aspirations and goals, often developed or refined with the help of AI writing tools.

W

• Well-Being Optimization (AI): Using AI-based insights and tools to improve mental, emotional, or physical health through data and automation.

Bibliography

A PA 7th Edition Format — Based exclusively on the manuscript content)

Brown, B. (2018). Dare to lead: Brave work. Tough conversations. Whole hearts. Random House.

Clear, J. (2018). Atomic habits: An easy & proven way to build good habits & break bad ones. Avery.

Dweck, C. S. (2006). Mindset: The new psychology of success. Random House.

Goleman, D. (1995). Emotional intelligence: Why it can matter more than IQ. Bantam Books.

Kahneman, D. (2011). Thinking, fast and slow. Farrar, Straus and Giroux.

Newport, C. (2016). Deep work: Rules for focused success in a distracted world. Grand Central Publishing.

Ries, E. (2011). The lean startup: How today's entrepreneurs use continuous innovation to create radically successful businesses. Crown Business.

Russell, S., & Norvig, P. (2020). Artificial intelligence: A modern approach (4th ed.). Pearson.

Seligman, M. E. P. (2011). Flourish: A visionary new understanding of happiness and well-being. Free Press.

Shneiderman, B. (2022). Human-centered AI. Oxford University Press.

Tegmark, M. (2017). Life 3.0: Being human in the age of artificial intelligence. Alfred A. Knopf.

Turkle, S. (2011). Alone together: Why we expect more from technology and less from each other. Basic Books.

Zuboff, S. (2019). The age of surveillance capitalism: The fight for a human future at the new frontier of power. PublicAffairs.

www.ingramcontent.com/pod-product-compliance
Lightning Source LLC
Chambersburg PA
CBHW071201120626
46546CB00006B/2359